INVESTMENT GUIDEBOOK FOR TEENS

2nd REVISED EDITION

THE ULTIMATE START TO GROWING YOUR WEALTH BEFORE 21 FROM BASICS TO BIG WINS IN STOCKS, BONDS, CRYPTO AND BEYOND

Emma Davis

Impact PUBLISHING

"Your thoughts shape your world. The mindset you choose today builds the life you'll live tomorrow."

NEW REVISED EDITION

Welcome to the New & Improved Edition!

We're so excited to share this updated edition with you! Thanks to your feedback, we've made your favorite book even **more engaging, enjoyable and easy to read.**

This edition strikes the right balance: **simple when it should be, detailed when it counts**. Not too much, not too little… just enough to keep teens learning and moving forward.

What's New in This Edition?

- Visuals that make lessons pop.
- Tips and takeaways to use right away.
- Quick activities to practice as you go.
- One chapter at a time, perfect for weekly reading.

TABLE OF CONTENTS

Quick Favor!

Your Review Makes a Difference

If you enjoy this book, please leave a review at emmadavisbooks.com or Amazon.com

SCAN ME

Your review helps us guide teens in the art of living—and gives parents the peace of mind they deserve.

Page Left Blank Intentionally

INTRODUCTION

Why Start Investing Before 21

> *"When money realizes that it is in good hands, it wants to stay and multiply in those hands."*
>
> **— Idowu Koyenikan**

GETTING STARTED WITH investing before you hit 21 may sound like an adult thing to do, but the truth is, it's one of the smartest moves you can make as a teenager or young adult. You might think investing is complicated, expensive, or even risky, but it doesn't have to be any of those. In fact, the earlier you begin, the easier and more powerful the journey becomes. There's a unique advantage young people have that can't be overstated: time. This book isn't about complex financial jargon or detailed strategies. Instead, it's about showing why starting now, right before or around adulthood, gives you a head start others wish they had.

When you're young, your time horizon is your biggest asset. Imagine planting a tree today versus planting it ten years from now. They're both investments in shade, oxygen, and beauty, but the tree planted today has a whole decade to grow strong and tall. Money works similarly. The sooner you start caring for it, the more chances it has to grow with you as your life and goals expand. Therefore, starting early is like giving your money the longest possible runway to take off.

Plus, investing young lets you learn through experience while you still have fewer responsibilities tying you down. Mistakes won't break you, and lessons hit home harder when you can apply them over the years rather than months. Some of the most important habits—like patience, discipline, and savvy decision-making—stick best when developed early. Even if you don't have a considerable amount to invest now, that's okay. Small amounts regularly invested can grow surprisingly large, especially when given time.

Another reason to begin investing before 21 is mindset. When young people start early, they embrace money as a tool, not just something to spend or stress over. Learning to see money as an opportunity builds confidence and opens doors to bigger goals like financial independence or freedom. This early relationship with money also challenges common myths about wealth and investing, helping you avoid traps many fall into later. Instead of money feeling scary or exclusive, it becomes approachable and manageable.

It's also important to realize that investing is about more than just buying stocks or chasing the latest crypto hype. At its core, investing means putting your money to work in ways that earn you more. This could be through stocks, bonds, real estate, or digital assets, but those details come later. Right now, understanding why earlier beats later sets the stage for everything else.

Once that clicks, financial independence stops feeling like a far-off fantasy. It becomes something you can actually reach. By the time your peers are juggling student loans, rent, or job uncertainty, you could already have a growing portfolio working in your favor. This doesn't mean you need to be rich overnight. Instead, you're building steady progress that feels more like a natural part of your life.

Besides financial reasons, early investing also builds critical skills that benefit other parts of life. Making financial decisions hones your ability to research, analyze risks, and think long term. It encourages curiosity and problem-solving while teaching patience and resisting the urge to seek instant gratification. These mental muscles carry over to school, relationships, and career. It's no coincidence that many successful entrepreneurs and professionals got comfortable managing risks and rewards early on.

Additionally, starting to invest young gives you the chance to take advantage of accounts designed for long-term growth. While you might not have access to these just yet, learning about them early means you'll be ready to use them when the time comes. Many tax-friendly accounts reward young investors by letting their money grow faster or be taxed at lower rates. The sooner you unlock these benefits, the more prosperous your future can be.

When you enter adulthood equipped with an investing habit, you're already ahead of the game. Most adults wish they had started earlier, but few take action to change it. You're in a unique position to build wealth without the pressure of heavy expenses or major financial commitments yet. Seeing your money grow, even gradually, builds motivation and pride. This positive feedback loop is what makes consistent early investing so effective.

On the flip side, the cost of waiting is enormous. Every year's delay can mean thousands of dollars in lost potential earnings. It's not just about missing gains but also about missing learning opportunities and building a sense of control. It's easy to convince yourself that saying "I'll start next year" or "when I have more money" is fine, but those delays add up quickly and set you behind later in life.

There's also a social aspect worth mentioning. Today, investing no longer fits the outdated stereotype of "old people's business." Teens and young adults are getting involved like never before, with accessible platforms and educational tools designed just for newcomers. This means you won't be alone. Many of your peers around the world are starting their investing journeys, sharing insights and growing their financial literacy together. You can be part of this positive movement that reshapes how young people think about money.

Starting before 21 also gives you freedom and options in the future. Instead of feeling forced to accept any job or pay simply to survive, investing early may help you build a safety net. This cushion can let you explore career paths you're passionate about—even if they don't pay much at first—or take risks like starting your own business. Investments grow quietly in the background, supporting your choices and reducing pressure.

So, if you've been wondering whether to jump into investing or wait until later, the strongest answer is this: the best time to start was yesterday, and the next best time is right now. You're human, learning as you go, and that's perfectly fine. This book will guide you every step of the way, showing you how to harness the power of early investing to build a wealthier, more confident future.

📖How to Get the Most Out of This Book: 5-Step Learning Path for Parents & Teens

Based on feedback from thousands of parents, the most effective way to help teens grow through reading is to keep it consistent, stress-free and fun. To help your teen get the most out of this book, here's the simple learning path that parents say works best:

Step 1: Read in Small Bites

Parents recommend reading 1–2 chapters per week. This pace keeps things manageable and prevents overwhelm for busy teens.

Step 2: Share Back Weekly

Encourage your teen to retell what they learned, either orally or in writing. This boosts confidence, strengthens communication skills, and helps you naturally see their progress.

Step 3: Read Together, Not Alone

Many parents find that reading side-by-side or aloud together creates bonding moments. Teens open up more when parents show genuine interest in the same material.

Step 4: Make It Fun & Rewarding

Small incentives go a long way. Parents say that weekly rewards (like a favorite snack or extra screen time) and bigger milestone rewards (like a gift card or outing) keep teens motivated and looking forward to reading.

Step 5: Celebrate, Don't Criticize

If a chapter feels "boring" or "difficult," break it down into short talks, connect the ideas to real life, and celebrate small wins. Teens don't need to ace every single chapter; just applying even one lesson makes a difference.

🌟 Encouragement

Remember, the goal isn't perfection. Just showing up consistently with your teen makes a lasting impact.

If your teen learns even one meaningful lesson from this book, that's a job well done! 👏

CHAPTER 1

Money Mindset: Why Teens Have the Biggest Advantage

> *"Your economic security does not lie in your job; it lies in your own power to produce—to think, to learn, to create, to adapt. That's true financial independence. It's not having wealth; it's having the power to produce wealth. It's intrinsic."*
>
> **—Stephen Covey**

STARTING TO THINK about money while you're still a teen gives you an edge that most adults no longer have, and that edge is time. When you begin early, even small amounts have room to grow alongside you. Good habits stack up, your confidence builds, and your money starts reflecting the choices you've been making all along. Teens also get to dodge common money myths that trap many adults, such as the idea that you need tons of cash to start investing. Your advantage isn't just in time or money, but in the chance to develop smart, lasting money habits before the noise and pressure of adult life pile on.

Therefore, this chapter aims to explore how your early choices create a financial head start that most people don't realize they missed until it's too late. So, let's dive in.

⏳ Time Is Your Superpower

If there's one thing that gives teens the ultimate edge in building financial independence, it's the incredible power of time. When you start developing strong money habits young, even small steps can grow into major long-term freedom because good choices stack on each other. Think of financial habits as decisions that build on past decisions, like a snowball rolling down a hill and getting bigger as it goes. The earlier you start, the more time your efforts have to grow, multiplying your progress in ways most people don't expect.

To understand this better, imagine setting aside even a small amount each week, learning how to manage your spending, or practicing a skill that can earn you money later. These actions might feel tiny now, but over the years, they add up to real financial strength. And if you wait until adulthood to begin, you lose years when these habits could have been building your confidence and stability. Time makes an enormous difference.

Now, why does starting young matter so much? It's because financial habits don't just add progress, they multiply it. When you're a teen, the foundation you build is only the beginning. Over time, the benefits of budgeting, saving, and learning financial basics support new opportunities. Each smart decision strengthens your future choices. This process repeats again and again, creating growth that feels powerful. But the key is patience and consistency. The longer you keep healthy money habits going, the more control and independence you gain.

Another advantage young people have is flexibility. Your timeline for reaching financial freedom is longer than that of adults who already have major expenses. This gives you room to experiment and learn without pressure. You can try different ways to earn, explore career interests, build skills, and figure out what kind of financial life you want. Even if some things don't work out, the long-term trend still moves you forward.

Financial habits also shape your mindset. Starting early teaches discipline because you get to watch small steps turn into real outcomes. That momentum builds confidence. Saving even a little, tracking where your money goes, or setting simple goals helps you gain control over your finances rather than feel controlled by them. These habits become the foundation for financial independence.

It might sound overwhelming to think about money when you're just starting out, especially if you don't have a job yet or earn very little. But the secret is simple: you don't need much to begin. Even small savings, mindful spending, or learning about money for a few minutes a day can create long-term growth. What matters most is starting early and sticking with it.

Here's something important: time can work against those who delay. Every year you wait to build good financial habits is a year of potential progress lost. It's easy to tell yourself you'll start "once you earn more."

But the truth is, the earlier you begin, the more room you give your skills and discipline to develop. If you're 15 now, taking small steps can lead to financial confidence and freedom much earlier in adulthood.

Compounding doesn't just apply to money; it applies to knowledge and skills, too. The sooner you start learning about budgeting, saving, earning, and smart spending, the more prepared you become for real-world decisions. This knowledge grows with you, giving you an advantage as you transition into adulthood. Your financial skills, like your habits, reward you more the earlier you develop them.

Because teens have the advantage of time, your mindset should shift from quick wins to long-term freedom. It's tempting to want instant results, but true financial independence comes from steady progress and smart choices over the years. It isn't about chasing expensive trends or trying to get rich fast. It's about building a lifestyle where you control your money, not the other way around.

And let's not forget emotional and financial resilience. As responsibilities increase, money management becomes essential. Building healthy financial habits early helps you stay ahead of stress. Consistency gives you stability and confidence, helping you face challenges with more clarity. Starting young gives you more time to strengthen these skills.

Fun Fact

With low-cost, digital investing tools now widely available, teens have more power than ever to start early, learn, and build wealth.

So, what's the takeaway? Don't let time slip away. Starting small, even if it feels insignificant, sets you up for success that grows year after year. This isn't magic or luck. It's consistent habits and smart decisions working together. Your greatest advantage is the time you have ahead of you. Use it well, and your financial independence will grow stronger than you can imagine.

The Difference Between Rich, Broke, and Wealthy Mindsets

Understanding money isn't just about knowing numbers or how much cash you have in your bank account. It's largely about the way you think and act around money—the mindset you carry every day. When it comes to money, people generally fall into three broad categories: rich mindset, broke mindset, and wealthy mindset. These aren't just labels about their bank accounts; these categories reveal very different approaches to money, risk, habits, and long-term success. Let's take a look at them:

Mindset	Focus	Typical Thoughts & Behaviors	Risks/Challenges
Broke Mindset 💸	Short-term money needs ⏳	Focuses on immediate expenses like bills, emergencies, and small purchases. Thoughts often include fear and scarcity, e.g., "What if I don't have enough next month?" 😟	Stuck in a cycle of living paycheck to paycheck, limited planning for the future, and avoiding calculated risks 🚫
Rich Mindset 💎	Income and consumption 💰	Ambitious about making money, status-driven, spends on lifestyle and luxury items. Examples: buying new gadgets yearly 📱, using credit to maintain image 💳	Often neglects security, savings, and investments; vulnerable to unexpected expenses or downturns ⚠️
Wealthy Mindset 🏦	Building and protecting lasting value 🌱	Focuses on growing, keeping, and reinvesting money. Emphasizes patience, smart decisions, and consistent habits over flashy purchases 🧠	Requires discipline and long-term planning; less focus on immediate gratification ⌛

Now, what does this look like in real life? Someone with a wealthy mindset saves regularly, invests early (even if the amounts are small), and thinks critically about risk. They avoid lifestyle inflation—the trap of spending more as their income grows—and aren't fooled by "get rich quick" schemes. Instead, they understand that wealth involves discipline, delayed gratification, and learning from mistakes. This mindset looks beyond money alone, recognizing that freedom and peace of mind are just as valuable.

Why does this matter, especially for teens? If you start with a wealthy mindset now, your financial trajectory changes entirely. Most adults start with either a broke or rich mindset and struggle to shift toward building real wealth later. But starting young, you don't have those ingrained habits yet. You have the advantage of molding your thinking early, which puts you ahead of the game. Time is your biggest ally, and the wealthy mindset harnesses that by focusing on the long game.

So, How Do These Mindsets Develop?

Experience plays a huge role, but so does environment—family conversations about money, friends' attitudes, and what you see on social media. Unfortunately, many people grow up surrounded by examples of the broke or rich mindset, rarely witnessing what a wealthy mindset looks like in action. This is why many teens get confused about money, equating wealth with buying expensive things quickly or feeling stuck worrying about debts and bills.

The wealthy mindset flips this script. It asks questions like, "How can I use my money to create more opportunities?" and "What choices can I make today to secure my future?" It values learning about money as a tool—whether through books, conversations, or real experiences like investing. It also understands that mistakes will happen, but each failure is a chance to get smarter and stronger, not a reason to give up.

Contrast that with the broken mindset's reaction to mistakes, which often involves shame, blame, or giving up because of fear. The rich mindset might push through mistakes, but only to earn or spend more, sometimes without a safety net or a real plan. The wealthy mindset takes a more strategic, emotionally steady approach, which is essential for long-term success.

Your mindset decides whether money controls you or empowers you.

For teens, the good news is this: your mindset is flexible. You're not locked into any one way of thinking. The wealthy mindset doesn't need you to have a huge allowance or a trust fund. It starts with small choices—saving a little of your earnings, prioritizing your financial education, and thinking about money as a tool to reach your bigger goals, not just as immediate cash to spend. This small daily shift, over months and years, becomes powerful. It's like planting seeds you don't see grow at first, but will become a forest later.

To sum it up, the **broke mindset** is about scarcity, present struggles, and reactive decisions. The **rich mindset** is about earning and spending, often focused on status and instant gratification. The **wealthy mindset** is about building lasting security, playing the long game, and making thoughtful, educated choices. The mindset you adopt shapes how you manage money, take risks, and respond to setbacks—everything that affects your financial future.

Getting familiar with these differences helps you recognize your own habits and beliefs. That awareness is the first step to changing your money story. It can be a little uncomfortable at first, challenging the reasons you spend or save the way you do. But over time, these shifts lead to confidence and freedom, not just in money, but in life.

In the upcoming chapters, you'll see how this mindset foundation supports everything else, from setting budgets and saving to investing and avoiding scams. The wealthy mindset isn't just a concept; it's a daily practice worth committing to now, while you have time on your side.

How Small Habits Beat Big One-Time Wins

When it comes to building wealth, the idea of striking it rich overnight is one that often grabs the spotlight. Everyone loves a good story about someone hitting a massive jackpot or making a fortune with a single investment. But here's the reality: those momentous wins are extremely rare, and relying on them is like expecting to ace a test without studying. For teens starting out, the power lies not in chasing the big one-time wins, but in building small, consistent habits that add up over time.

Small habits might sound boring or insignificant at first, especially when compared to flashy success stories. But the truth is that they form the foundation for long-term financial independence. Think of them like baby steps toward a giant mountain. Each step isn't a headline, but it's what eventually gets you to the peak. Teens have a unique advantage here because the earlier you start, the more those small habits compound, growing quietly but powerfully in the background.

🏆 Building Discipline, Confidence, and Consistency

Imagine setting aside just $5 a day or establishing a weekly routine to review your spending and savings goals. These actions may seem tiny, especially in a world where people flaunt overnight successes or viral social media riches. However, establishing such habits early on trains your brain and your money to work together. It turns investing and saving into something regular and automatic, rather than a one-off event you "maybe try" once and then forget about.

One big reason why small habits beat big one-time wins is consistency. When you consistently save even small amounts, your money benefits not only from your contributions but also from compound growth. Teens can leverage consistency to develop discipline—one of the most critical ingredients for any financial success. Discipline built through small wins every day translates into the ability to stick with budgets, avoid unnecessary debt, and steadily invest for the future. If you wait for the "perfect moment" or a "big break," you risk never taking the first step, or worse, chasing risky ideas that can drag you down.

Another often overlooked point about small habits is how they build confidence. When you see your savings account grow week after week or get comfortable setting up automatic transfers, it gives you a sense of control over your finances. This confidence makes you less likely to fall for scams, impulsive buying, or hyped-up "get rich quick" schemes. Confidence grows in those small moments of success and helps you make smarter money decisions as you go.

Take the example of investing. Instead of waiting to save thousands of dollars before buying your first stock or crypto asset, habitually invest small amounts, like $20 every month, to build familiarity and remove the fear. You learn how the market behaves without overwhelming yourself. Those first small investments teach patience. You see the ups and downs, the dips and rallies, and understand that wealth is a marathon, not a sprint. All because you practiced a simple habit of starting early and staying consistent.

Small habits also help you avoid the emotional rollercoasters that big one-time wins or losses often bring. If you suddenly make or lose a large sum of money, emotions such as excitement, fear, or panic can lead to poor decisions. When you've built up your money steadily, you experience fewer shocks and a smoother relationship with your finances. This steadiness is invaluable because it encourages clear thinking and long-term focus.

💰 Making Money Management Simple and Scalable

Moreover, small habits make money management feel less intimidating. Let's be honest: when you're new to money stuff, it can seem complicated with all the jargon, charts, and advice out there. But if you start with easy, manageable actions—checking your bank balance regularly, saving a tiny percentage of your income, or learning the basics of investing through small trades—you change your mindset. Money stops being this huge, mysterious thing and instead becomes something you control step by step.

One powerful small habit to develop is "learning a little every day." Instead of trying to understand everything about investing or personal finance all at once, commit to discovering small nuggets of knowledge regularly. This could be as simple as reading a short article or watching a five-minute video about budgeting or investing strategies. Over time, these tiny bursts of learning build a strong knowledge base without overwhelming you. Pretending you have to learn it all at once often leaves you feeling lost and leads to quitting.

The impact of these small habits stacks not just financially, but mentally as well. Winning small battles in your money life improves your financial self-discipline, reduces stress, and builds optimism about your future. This positive feedback loop is crucial as you get older and face larger financial challenges, such as college expenses, rent, or a car payment. Your small habits give you tools to tackle these moments rather than panic.

One common misconception teens have is that if they slip up or miss a day or a week of saving or learning, it's game over. In reality, small habits are forgiving because they're designed to be done over and over again, regardless of how many times you stumble. The key is getting back on track quickly and not letting perfection or failure stop you. Just like physical fitness, a missed day doesn't ruin your progress if you keep moving forward.

Another advantage of small habits is how they scale with your income and goals. For example, when you land your first job or start making money from a side hustle, those habits translate well to bigger opportunities. Saving 10% of $20 is great practice for saving 10% of $500. By mastering habits early, you're ready to handle more complex financial moves like tax planning, larger investments, or budgeting for big purchases without losing control.

🧘 Patience Pays: Small Habits, Big Wins

Small habits also encourage patience—the most underrated money skill. Patience means accepting that wealth won't be built in a day and that learning to manage money is an ongoing process. Patience drives you to keep investing, saving, and learning, even when the results aren't instantly visible. As a teen, you have this advantage naturally, as time plays in your favor, letting patience work magic through compound interest and repeated actions.

The reality is that big one-time wins often come with big risks. Many teens hear stories of a kid making thousands from a viral NFT drop or a crypto coin exploding overnight and get hooked on finding the next "big thing." But often, those big wins come with high chances of losing everything just as fast. Sticking with small, steady habits reduces risk and builds a resilient foundation, giving you control rather than wild guesses.

Reflect on habits like regularly checking your spending to avoid leaking money on small, unnoticed purchases or setting up a monthly transfer to your investment account without thinking. These small actions help you build an automatic system for financial growth. Over months and years, money habits turn into lifestyle habits. You don't have to think about saving or investing; it happens as naturally as brushing your teeth or eating breakfast.

In the end, what matters most isn't how much money you start with, but how reliable and sustainable your money habits are. Rather than waiting for a lottery ticket win or a lucky stock pick, the smartest move is to develop habits that keep your financial engine running every day. Those daily choices add up to a snowball effect that can turn handfuls of dollars into real wealth. This mindset—focused on small wins—is what puts teens in a powerful position to outpace older investors who might be stuck chasing flashy but risky moves.

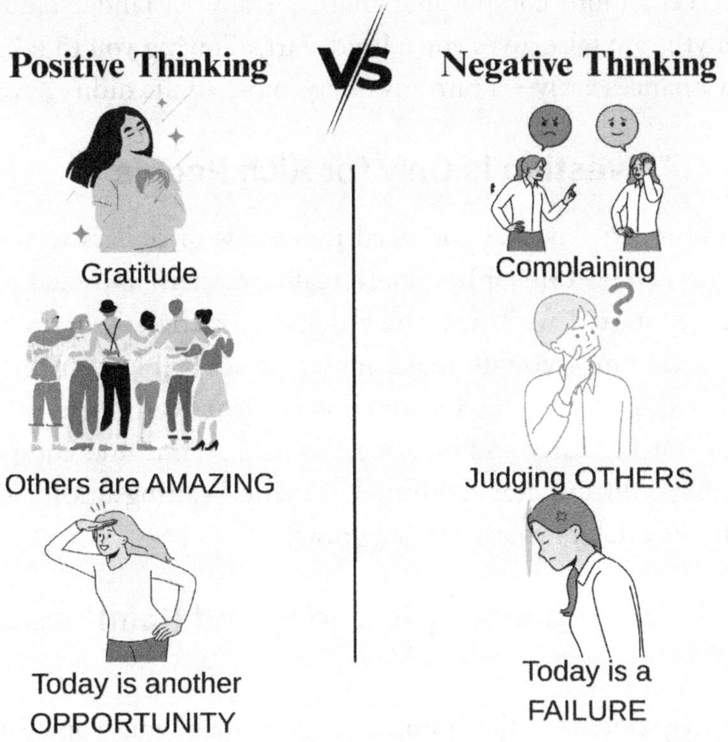

So, focus on what you can control: your actions today. Create the habit of saving, investing, and learning regularly. Celebrate the small victories, because they're the building blocks of big success. Time is your biggest ally, and those daily steps, even if tiny, will keep you moving steadily toward financial independence.

Common Teen Money Myths and Why They're Wrong

Many teens inherit misconceptions about money that can hold them back before they even get started. These myths aren't harmless because they can shape how you think about earning, saving, and investing for years. Some create unnecessary fear or frustration, making managing money seem more complicated than it really is. Understanding why these myths are false gives you a head start, allowing you to take control of your finances early—a rare advantage most adults didn't have.

Myth 1: "Investing is Only for Rich People"

A common belief is that you need thousands of dollars to invest. For teens, this can be a major barrier. In reality, modern apps and platforms let you get started with just a few dollars. Fractional shares and low- or no-minimum accounts make investing accessible even on a small allowance or part-time job income. The key isn't how much you invest at first; it's starting early and building the habit. Time and compounding do the heavy lifting, not the initial amount. Waiting until you're "rich enough" only delays your financial growth.

Myth 2: "Saving Money is Boring and Pointless as a Teen"

Saving may not have the immediate thrill of buying something new, but it's far from pointless. Developing the habit of consistently setting money aside, even in small amounts, builds a cushion for the future. This foundation reduces stress when taking risks or investing later because you have a backup. Saving quietly fuels the flashy financial wins that come later, making it one of the most powerful tools for long-term economic independence.

Myth 3: "Budgeting Means Giving Up Fun"

Many teens assume budgeting is restrictive. In truth, it's about making conscious choices, balancing priorities, and planning for fun without guilt. When done right, budgeting empowers you to spend intentionally, enjoy life, and avoid running empty. It's not a punishment; it's a tool that puts you in control.

Myth 4: "Debt is Always Bad"

Not all debt is harmful. While high-interest credit card debt can be dangerous, other forms—like student loans—can be investments in your future earning potential. Learning the difference early gives you a huge advantage. The key is knowing when debt is a tool and when it's a trap. Avoiding all debt blindly may feel safe, but it can limit your options in the long term.

Myth 5: "I'm Too Young to Mess Up Money Decisions"

Many teens believe their financial mistakes won't matter or mean failure. In reality, starting young gives you the freedom to learn from small mistakes while the stakes are low. Everyone slips up with money—even adults. Learning early helps you understand budgeting, saving, and investing before handling larger sums, giving you a safer, more confident start.

Fun Fact

Young investors can afford to take more risks because they have decades to recover from market downturns.

Myth 6: "Making Money is Just About Luck"

Success isn't purely luck or connections. While being in the right place at the right time helps, consistent money skills—saving, budgeting, earning, and investing—prepare you to seize opportunities when they arise. Reliance on luck often leads to chasing risky schemes, but steady habits build real financial opportunities.

Myth 7: "Investing is Too Risky Without a Safety Net"

Fear of investing is common, especially with stories of market crashes or scams. While investing carries risks, avoiding it completely is often worse. Knowledge, diversification, and starting small make risk manageable. Being young works in your favor—time smooths out market fluctuations, and early experience compounds growth over the years.

Myth 8: "You Have to Understand Everything Before You Start"

No one masters money perfectly. Learning is ongoing, and the sooner you start practicing, the faster you gain experience. Waiting until you feel 100% ready usually means waiting too long. Every small effort now adds up, and mistakes teach valuable lessons that accelerate your understanding.

Myth 9: "Making Tons of Money Fast Builds Real Wealth"

Quick wins or viral success stories are rare. Relying on them often leads to risky behavior or scams. Real wealth grows through steady effort, good habits, and patience. Consistent saving and investing work quietly, compounding over time. Teen years are the perfect window to develop these habits and build a strong financial foundation.

Myth 10: "Money Management is Boring and Only for Adults"

Many teens see money as stressful or dull, but mastering it unlocks freedom, control, and future choices. Teen years are ideal for experimenting because mistakes are smaller and the stakes are lower. Tracking savings, hitting financial goals, or making your first investment is motivating and even fun. Money skills aren't just numbers—they're tools to design the life you want.

In summation, these myths create unnecessary barriers that delay teens from saving, investing, and making smart financial decisions. The truth is encouraging and straightforward: you don't need a ton of cash, perfect knowledge, or adult-level experience to start building wealth. Rejecting these myths and adopting a proactive money mindset turns your teen years into a powerful growth period, setting the stage for lifelong financial independence. Your advantage isn't handling huge sums now—it's learning, practicing, and thinking differently about money while time works in your favor.

📌 Final Thoughts

Starting early gives you a unique edge because you have time. Even small habits such as saving, investing, and tracking spending add up over the years into real financial strength. Your advantage is not how much money you start with but the mindset, discipline, and confidence you build now.

Parents' Corner

Take a "Money Walk" together. Go for a short walk while discussing a simple money topic such as saving goals, a recent purchase, or a small investment idea. Walking keeps the conversation relaxed and makes learning about money feel natural, active, and stress-free.

Focus on consistent, smart choices, challenge common money myths, and let patience guide you. Every step you take shapes not just your finances but the life you will create. Start today because time is on your side.

Key Takeaways

- **Time is Your Superpower:** Starting early gives you a huge advantage because your money and habits have years to grow. Even small amounts of saving or investing can multiply over time through compounding.
- **Small Habits Build Big Results:** Consistent daily or weekly actions, such as saving, tracking spending, or learning about money, build long-term financial strength. These habits are more reliable than chasing one-time windfalls.
- **Mindset Shapes Your Financial Future:** How you think about money matters more than how much you start with. A wealthy mindset focuses on growth, patience, and smart decisions rather than instant gratification or flashy spending.
- **Patience and Consistency Beat Quick Wins:** Quick financial gains are rare and risky. Steady, disciplined habits over months and years provide stability, confidence, and resilience that shortcuts cannot match.
- **Challenging Myths Prevents Setbacks:** Believing that investing is only for the rich, budgeting is boring, or debt is always bad can hold you back. Understanding the truth behind these myths allows you to act wisely from the start.
- **Early Learning Builds Confidence and Control:** Developing money skills and experimenting with small financial decisions now gives you control over your finances, reducing stress and preparing you for bigger challenges in adulthood.

Journal Activity

Use this activity to reflect on your money mindset, track your habits, and plan small steps toward financial independence. Take a few minutes each day or each week to think or write.

- What money-related choices did I make today? How did they make me feel?
- What small financial action did I take this week, even if it was tiny?
- What did I learn about money, saving, or investing this week?
- What is one money goal I want to focus on next week?
- Did I notice any money myths or fears influencing my choices? How can I challenge them?

🎓 Exercise: "Money Mission Challenge"

Turn building financial habits into a mini-game to practice consistency, mindset, and small wins.

Step 1: Set Your Mission

- ☐ Pick a small financial goal for the week. Examples:
- ☐ Save $5 every day
- ☐ Track all spending for one week
- ☐ Learn one new thing about investing
- ☐ Write your mission at the top of your page.

Step 2: Daily Money Missions

- Each day, complete one small action toward your goal. Some ideas:
- Transfer a small amount to savings
- Check your bank balance and review spending
- Watch a short video or read an article about money

Step 3: Record Your Wins

Use the lines below to write one sentence per day about what you did, how it felt, and any lessons learned.

____

____

____

____

Step 4: Reward Yourself

At the end of the week, celebrate completing your mission. Rewards could be simple: a fun snack, a walk with friends, or a small treat.

CHAPTER 2

First Steps to Wealth: Goals, Budgets & Emergency Cash

> ***"A budget is more than just a series of numbers on a page; it is an embodiment of our values."***
>
> **—Barack Obama**

STARTING YOUR JOURNEY to wealth means getting crystal clear on what you want, how you'll manage the money coming in and going out, and having a safety net ready for the unexpected. Setting specific money goals gives you a target to aim for, whether it's saving for college, a car, or your first investment. From there, creating a budget that separates needs, wants, and fun money helps you control your spending without feeling trapped. And while it might sound boring, building even a small emergency cash stash can save you from scrambling when life throws a curveball, like laptop repairs or last-minute expenses.

These first steps might feel basic, but they're the foundation everyone who builds real wealth starts with—and getting them right early makes everything else easier down the road, and this chapter is all about creating that foundation.

Dream Life by 30: Turning Vibes into Clear Money Goals

So, you've heard people say it before—"Set your goals early." But what does that really mean, especially when you're just starting out with money? The idea of a "dream life" sounds kind of like a vibe, something you feel more than can touch. Maybe you picture traveling the world, buying your first car without stressing, or having the freedom to stay home and work on your passion projects. But as awesome as those dreams are, the jump from vague vibes to actual dollars and cents takes some focus and planning. Getting clear about what you want money to do for you isn't just about daydreaming; it's about turning those vibes into real, measurable goals you can chase with purpose.

Investor's Mindset Check

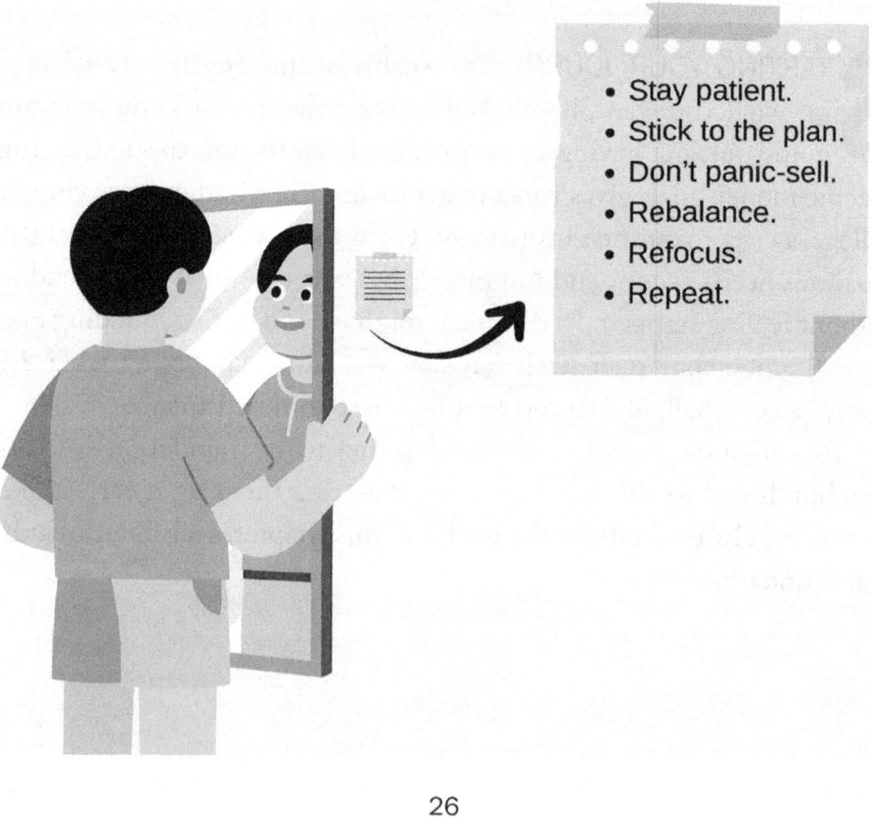

Breakdown Huge Goals into Measurable Steps

Imagine sitting down with a notepad or your phone and writing out what your ideal life looks like at 30. Don't just say, "I want to be rich." That's too broad. Instead, try breaking it down: Where will you live? Will you rent or own a place? What kind of car do you want, if any? What hobbies or experiences do you want to pursue? When you get specific, you start to create a mental blueprint. This helps you figure out how much money you'll actually need to make those things possible, and more importantly, how much you have to save and invest to get there.

One of the biggest mistakes teens make is treating money as either an endless resource or something that magically appears when needed. Your "dream life" won't just fall into your lap; it requires a roadmap. And that roadmap needs clear checkpoints: monthly savings targets, investment goals, and even timelines for milestones like buying a car or funding a trip abroad. When your goals have timelines, they become more real, and that urgency can be exactly what drives you to save or invest, even when it feels tough.

Here's a secret: most people don't get rich because they make big, flashy moves. They get rich by figuring out what their dream life means in dollars, then working backward, month by month, year by year. Say you want $500,000 by 30 to cover a down payment on a house or to have enough invested for financial freedom. That sounds huge, right? But when you break it down—say, investing $400 a month starting at 18—you start to see a doable path. It moves from being a mystical fantasy to an actual plan you can follow.

Align Your Goals to Your Values

Another key part of this is understanding that your goals should reflect what matters most to **you**. Some people want a fancy car; others want to launch a side business or travel for months. No goals are right or wrong; they just have to be personal. If your goals don't connect to your core values, you're less likely to stick to the money plan that gets you there.

Your "vibes" are your motivators, but clear money goals turn motivation into action.

> **Fun Fact**
>
> Visualizing your average day at age 30 helps clarify the kind of financial life you want, making your goals more meaningful and easier to act on. When you have a strong reason behind your financial choices, you're far more likely to stay consistent and motivated than if you rely on short bursts of inspiration.

Don't worry if you're not sure exactly what your dream life looks like today; it evolves as you grow and learn. But starting the practice of translating feelings into numbers right now creates habits that last a lifetime. Say you jot down, "I want to be able to afford a plane ticket home without stressing." That might turn into a goal of saving $1,000 in an emergency fund, which then helps you build the discipline to save for bigger goals later.

Once you've got a clearer picture, it's time to prioritize. Maybe you want to travel the world, but also want to buy a car. Which one should come first? Sometimes, your goals will compete for the same dollars, and picking priorities keeps you from chasing too many things at once and getting overwhelmed. The beauty of starting young, though, is having the luxury of time. You can sequence your goals, tackling some now and others down the line, without sacrificing too much of either dream.

Be Honest

Turning vibes into money goals requires honesty, especially about your current financial situation. Be real about your income, your expenses, and what you can realistically save or invest. Stretch goals are reasonable; they push you, but setting impossible targets leads to burnout. Remember, the goal isn't to be perfect, it's to start.

Still, don't let imperfection freeze you. It's much better to start with a goal that's "good enough" and adjust as you go than to wait until you feel totally prepared. Life changes, and so will your circumstances. Maybe you find a new passion or make a side hustle that boosts your income. Goals aren't set in stone; they're directions, not destinations.

One practical tip for keeping those money goals front and center is to write them down visibly—on your phone's notes, on a wall calendar, or in a journal. Regularly reviewing your goals makes them feel alive. Each month, check in: Did you hit your savings target? What's one small step you can take to get closer? These tiny course corrections keep you moving forward, and they build your confidence.

🌱 Emotions and Money Go Hand in Hand

Let's talk about vibes for a second because that's the fuel behind your goals. It might seem silly to put "vibes" and "money" in the same sentence, but emotions and values actually play a huge role in why money habits stick or fail. If your dream life is about freedom, space, and creativity, then your goals to save and invest aren't just about numbers; they're about buying yourself options in the future. That emotional connection helps you resist impulse buys or the pressure to spend on "status" stuff before you're ready.

Another way to solidify your dreams is by linking your money goals to things you truly love. If you want to be a creator one day, maybe your goal isn't just "save money," but "invest in better gear" or "fund a small online store." When money goals connect to your passions, it's easier to stay consistent because you're working toward what lights you up. Personal meaning makes the grind feel less like a chore.

Build Clear Goals

Turning your dream life into clear goals also saves you from one big trap: drifting without direction. When money is just "whatever's left over," it can disappear fast. Setting concrete targets rewires your brain to think ahead and make smarter decisions. Over time, these mental shifts lead to healthier habits and a mindset where investing and saving aren't boring chores but stepping stones.

And here's something that might surprise you: your goals don't have to be giant ambitions right out of the gate. Maybe your first money goal is just building a $500 emergency fund or learning how to automate a small monthly investment. Those things might feel small now, but they build essential muscles—discipline, awareness, and confidence—that pay off massively later.

Remember, your dream life by 30 is your unique masterpiece. No one else's dreams have to look like yours. Clear money goals give you the power to write that story on your own terms. So start by capturing those vibes, turn them into dollars and dates, and let that clarity guide you. The more tangible your money goals become, the more unstoppable you'll be as you build a future that's not just rich in cash, but rich in purpose and freedom.

💳 Simple Teen Budget: Needs, Wants, and Fun Money

Starting to manage your money with a clear budget might sound boring, but it actually gives you more freedom and control than you imagine. When you're a teen learning about investing and building wealth, setting up a simple budget is the foundation for everything that comes next. Budgeting isn't about restricting yourself forever; it's about knowing where your money goes and making smart choices so you can save, invest, and still enjoy life. The easiest way to get started is by dividing your money into three categories: needs, wants, and fun money.

Think of needs as the essentials — stuff you absolutely have to pay for, like transportation to school or work, basic phone bills, even saving a little toward personal hygiene products. These are things that keep your daily life running smoothly. While some teens might think their needs are more than they actually are, getting clear on what truly counts as a need is important. For example, eating out regularly might feel like a need, but cooking at home or packing a lunch usually costs less and still keeps you fueled. Of course, not every expense fits neatly into needs. That's where wants and fun money come into play.

Needs vs. Wants

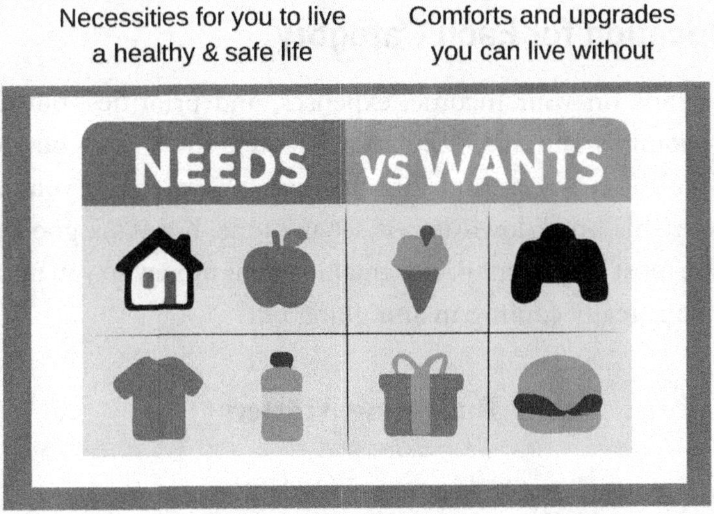

Adapted from HOWTOMONEY.com

Wants are the things you don't have to have but really want to have, like new clothes, trendy gadgets, or the latest video game. They're fun and often feel urgent, but they're different from needs because they don't keep you alive or functioning day to day. Learning to separate wants from needs is a skill that protects your savings and investments. If you find yourself spending most of your money on wants, it's going to be much harder to build wealth or even save for an emergency fund. By consciously deciding which wants are worth it and which aren't, you can enjoy without going broke.

Fun money is the smaller, guilt-free portion of your budget that you set aside for spontaneous or just "for fun" purchases—maybe grabbing an afternoon coffee with friends or going to a movie. This money is important because it helps savings feel less like a punishment. Think of it as your financial breathing room. Fun money helps you stick to your budget long-term because, let's face it, nobody wants to feel like they're living in a financial prison. Having a regular allowance for fun purchases means you can recharge and reward yourself without messing up your bigger goals.

Allocation for Each Category

That depends on your income, expenses, and priorities, but a simple starting point is the 50/30/20 rule adapted for a teen budget: 50% to needs, 30% to wants, and 20% to fun—or savings, if you're feeling ambitious. This breakdown is not set in stone, but it's a good place to begin. The most important part is tracking your money so you understand how much is really coming in and going out.

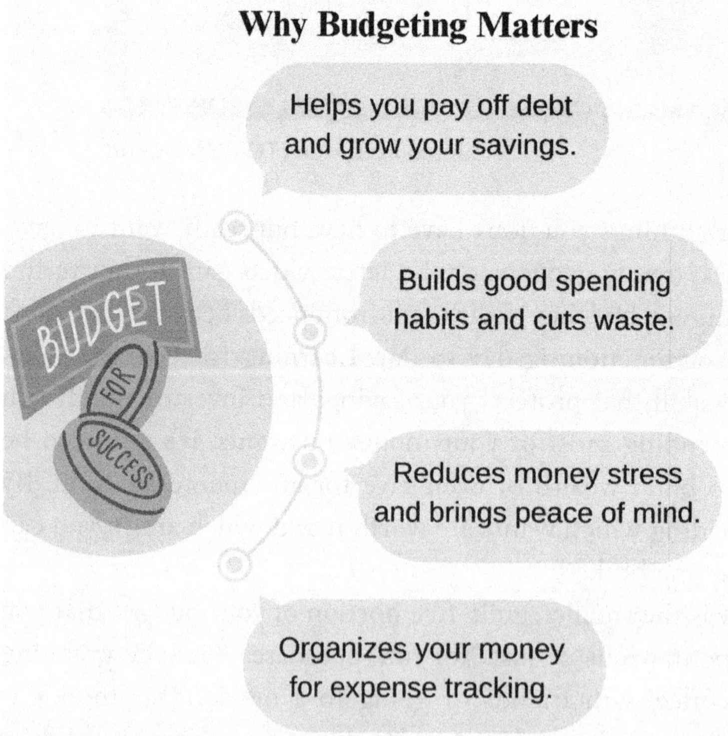

Tracking your spending doesn't require complicated apps or financial software. You can use simple tools like notes on your phone or a basic spreadsheet. Write down each purchase right after it happens, or set aside five minutes daily to update your spending log. Doing this regularly gives you a clear picture of where any leaks might be — maybe you're spending too much on snacks or online games without realizing it. Once you're aware, you can decide whether to cut back in certain areas and shift money toward savings or investment goals.

Budgeting as a Habit and Goal-Driven Tool

Budgeting is also about habits. The earlier you make it a habit to check in with your money, whether that's weekly or monthly, the more natural managing your finances will feel in the long run. It's like brushing your teeth, but for your wallet. This way, you can tweak your allocations as your needs change, your income grows, or new opportunities arise.

Another point to consider is how budgeting connects with your goals. Let's say you want to save for your first investment account or buy a new laptop for school or work. Your budget should reflect those priorities. Fun money is great, but if you're waiting on a financial milestone to unlock the future you want, sometimes tightening the fun money category for a few months can accelerate your progress. On the flip side, if you're too strict, you risk burning out and abandoning your plan altogether. The best budgets are flexible, realistic, and tailored to you.

Most teens don't have a simple, fixed income like a full-time job paycheck, but rather an inconsistent income from part-time jobs, allowances, or side hustles. This up-and-down cash flow makes budgeting a bit trickier but not impossible. In months where you bring in extra, try to boost your savings or fun money. And in tighter months, prioritize your needs first, then your wants, and temporarily reduce fun money. The goal is to avoid overdrawing or feeling stressed every time your money changes. Over time, this awareness builds financial resilience, so you're better prepared to handle bigger financial ups and downs as an adult.

One significant advantage of starting your budget early is learning to make financial choices before bigger responsibilities arise. College, rent, transportation, and higher bills often come with adult life, but when you've already nailed down how to allocate money, you won't be caught off guard. Plus, the discipline you develop in managing small amounts early on naturally extends to managing larger sums, investment accounts, and eventually real wealth.

Finally, remember that a simple budget isn't about perfection. You'll make mistakes and occasionally overspend on wants or fun money, and that's okay. The difference comes in recognizing those moments without guilt and using them as chances to refine your system. Your first budget probably won't be perfect, and it doesn't need to be. What counts is starting, adjusting, and sticking with it consistently over time.

So before diving deep into stocks, bonds, or crypto, make sure your foundation is solid. Build a simple budget that tells your needs apart from your wants, and don't forget to carve out some fun money. With clear categories and disciplined tracking, you'll not only control your spending but also create the space needed to save and invest early. This combination practically guarantees future wealth-building success.

Building a Starter Emergency Fund Even If You're Broke

Starting an emergency fund might feel impossible when you're broke or barely scraping by, but it's one of the smartest moves you can make to protect your future. Life doesn't always go as planned. Phones break, unexpected bills pop up, or maybe you suddenly lose a source of income. An emergency fund acts like a financial safety net, giving you a buffer to handle these surprises without stress or debt. Even if your bank account is nearly empty now, establishing this fund, no matter how small, is crucial. It's about building a habit of saving and laying a foundation for lifelong wealth.

The common misconception is that you need hundreds or thousands of dollars saved before an emergency fund "counts." The truth? It's okay to start with just $100 or even $25. The goal isn't to have a perfect fund overnight but to get the ball rolling so the idea of emergency savings becomes part of your money mindset. Every dollar you tuck away is a victory. This small initial cushion makes a huge difference by training you to prioritize saving and helping you avoid bad choices, like relying on credit cards or loans when trouble hits.

Let's break down why this matters, especially for teens or young adults just starting out. You're at an age where expenses are starting to pop up—maybe buying groceries, paying for phone plans, transit, or saving for your first car. You probably don't have a steady, big paycheck yet, and that's okay. You might even be juggling school, part-time work, or side gigs. That means your income can be unstable or irregular. When that happens, having any amount of emergency cash can prevent a small mishap from turning into a big financial crisis.

Think about it like this: if you get a flat tire or your phone suddenly dies, and you have $50 set aside, you won't have to borrow from your friends or family or fall behind on payments. That $50 is freedom. It's independence. It relieves the immediate financial strain and gives you more control. And controlling your money is precisely what builds confidence and wealth over time.

But how do you build this fund if you don't have much income to start with? Here are some practical steps that work even when your cash flow feels tight:

- **Set a tiny, achievable goal.** Instead of aiming for $1,000 or $500 right off the bat, pick something manageable like $25 or $50. You might be surprised how quickly small goals get met when you focus on just one milestone at a time.
- **Break it down into bite-sized amounts.** If getting $25 in a single week feels hard, try saving $5 each day from whatever income you get—whether it's allowance, tips, or earnings from a quick gig.

- **Use cash envelopes or separate accounts.** Physically separating your emergency fund money, even if it's just a few dollars, will help you avoid the temptation to spend it accidentally.
- **Automate when you can.** If you receive a small paycheck, set up an automatic transfer of even $5 to a savings account so the money moves before you have a chance to spend it.
- **Find windfalls and stash them.** Got birthday money, cash gifts, or some unexpected income? Please resist the urge to splurge and direct at least part of it to your emergency fund.

The idea is simple: make saving feel normal and doable instead of overwhelming. Your emergency fund doesn't need to solve all your money problems right away, but it does need to start somewhere. This mindset shift—seeing saving as a priority no matter what—will grow into something powerful.

Remember, emergencies don't ask for your permission before they come. They also don't care how old you are or how much money you have. Having this safety net, even in the early stages, prevents you from falling into the dangerous cycle of borrowing or relying on high-interest debt to cover basic needs. Credit cards might sound like easy solutions when you're short on cash, but they come with traps that keep you broke much longer than you realize.

Also, saving for emergencies builds discipline and patience, two qualities that pay off in investing and wealth creation, too. It trains you to prioritize long-term security over instant gratification. And that's a mindset that will continue to serve you as your income grows and you start tackling bigger financial goals like building a portfolio or buying your first car.

Consider a real-life example: a young teenager working a weekend job saves $10 a week. That's just $40 a month. In six months, they have $240 in their emergency fund. That won't cover everything if something big happens, but it could pay to fix a phone screen, replace lost headphones, or cover transport to an important event. Having that money ready means less panic and more flexibility. Then, as income improves—maybe with a raise or a new gig—the person can increase how much they save each month, growing the fund to eventually cover 3 to 6 months' worth of essential expenses.

What about when you don't have any steady income? Maybe you're saving money from allowances or the occasional paid chore. The key is not to wait for perfect circumstances. Start now with whatever you get. The habit you build, even with tiny contributions, matters far more than the amount. It's putting consistency over perfection.

> **Fun Fact**
>
> An emergency fund isn't a dull side task; it's your first real financial asset. Having cash set aside creates a safety buffer that makes it easier to take smart risks later. With a reliable backup for unexpected expenses, you can invest consistently and confidently without the stress of "what if" holding you back.

Some people think emergencies are rare or "don't happen to them," especially when they're young. But the truth is, everyone faces unexpected expenses at some point, and younger people often do so without a financial cushion. That's what makes this step so important early in life: getting comfortable with setting money aside builds resilience. When you naturally handle small emergencies without panicking, you'll get used to managing bigger money responsibilities more calmly in the future.

Here's a quick checklist to summarize how to get started with your emergency fund right now:

- ☐ Start with a small, specific target like $25 or $50.
- ☐ Save a little bit regularly, even a few dollars a week.
- ☐ Use a separate savings account or a dedicated place (digital or physical).
- ☐ Automate transfers if you can, even if it's a tiny amount.
- ☐ Put unexpected money (gifts, bonuses) straight into your fund instead of spending it.
- ☐ Focus on building the habit long before chasing a big balance.

It's okay if your emergency fund takes months or even years to reach a full safety level. What matters is building momentum and staying consistent. Like with investing, the earliest step is often the hardest, but it sets up everything that follows.

Financial emergencies can leave you vulnerable, but having a starter emergency fund gives you the freedom and stability you need. It'll stop money stress from overwhelming every decision and start turning money from a worry into a tool. And that's where real financial freedom begins, by protecting yourself first so you can take bigger steps toward your money goals without fear.

Fun Fact:
People who write down their budgets are 42% more likely to achieve their financial goals!

Money Tracking Made Easy: Apps, Notes, or Spreadsheets

Once you've set clear money goals, created a simple budget, and started building your emergency fund, the next big step is keeping track of where your money goes. It sounds basic, but tracking your income and expenses is the foundation of any serious money plan. Without it, you're basically flying blind. Kids and young adults often think managing money means just 'not spending too much,' but the truth is that knowing exactly how much you earn and spend every week or month gives you power. It tells you what's working, what needs to change, and where you can squeeze out savings to invest in your future.

The good news is that money tracking doesn't have to be complicated or time-consuming. You don't need fancy tools or accounting degrees. Instead, there are three straightforward ways to get started: using apps on your phone, simple notes (digital or paper), or good old spreadsheets. Each method has pros and cons, so choosing the right one depends on your personality, habits, and goals.

🌐 Apps

Apps are probably the most popular option among teens since smartphones are everywhere. They automate a lot of the work by linking to your bank account or debit card, automatically categorizing your spending, and showing you real-time snapshots of your finances. That makes apps feel like magic because, with little effort, you get clear visuals of where your money goes every week or month. Plus, many apps can set spending limits, track savings goals, and even remind you when bills are due to avoid late fees.

However, apps don't work perfectly for everyone. Some teens dislike letting an app access their bank accounts, or they might get overwhelmed by so many features. Also, automatic categorization isn't always accurate; you might have to correct or tweak categories, like changing "entertainment" to "fun money." But if you want a low-effort way to keep tabs on spending and saving, starting with a trusted app is a smart move.

📄 Notes

If you'd rather keep things old-school, simple notes can be surprisingly effective. This method means jotting down every time you earn or spend money, whether in a notebook or a notes app on your phone. It takes more discipline because you have to remember to write things down, but that act of logging transactions sharpens your awareness. You start noticing patterns like how much a daily coffee or weekend event really costs, which can add up fast.

Using notes is also perfect if you don't have a bank account yet or prefer to handle cash. Writing things out connects you more directly with your money decisions than just tapping buttons on a screen. You can organize your notes by day or week and add quick reflections, like "Maybe don't buy snacks this often" or "Save part of this paycheck." If you like pen and paper or digital lists, this simple approach still works great to keep you accountable.

📈 Spreadsheets

The final option is spreadsheets, which might sound more complex than it is. Programs like Google Sheets or Excel let you build a simple table with your income on one side, spending categories on the other, and calculations that automatically sum totals and track progress. Spreadsheets give you full control over how detailed you want to be and allow you to customize them as your needs evolve—plus, they create a digital history of your money habits.

A smart budget balances fun today and freedom tomorrow.

Many young investors eventually migrate to spreadsheets because they combine flexibility, control, and clarity. Unlike automatic apps, you decide how to break down your spending categories, whether it's "rent," "subscriptions," or "fun money." You also get practice organizing data—a skill that's useful in many life areas beyond finance. Starting small with a basic income vs. expenses tracker is enough; no need to create a complicated financial model.

It's important to pick a system you'll actually stick with. If apps feel intrusive or overwhelming, go simple with notes or spreadsheets. If you forget to jot down every expense, an app's reminders and automatic tracking might be better. No method is perfect; what matters is creating the habit of checking in regularly, whether it's daily, weekly, or when you get paid. Consistency builds awareness, and awareness builds control.

Tracking Money and Stopping Leaks

Another benefit of regular money tracking is spotting leaks—those small, sneaky expenses that quietly drain your cash. Teens often underestimate how much they spend on small purchases like gaming skins, snacks, or subscriptions they barely use. Tracking highlights these habits, helping you decide whether certain spending aligns with your long-term goals or if there's room to cut back. Those savings can turn into extra money to put into your emergency fund or start investing.

Tracking also shines brightest when paired with reflection. It's not just about numbers on a screen or page; it's about asking, "Why did I spend this?" "Was it worth it?" or "Could I have gotten the same joy for less?" This mindset turns tracking from a chore into a discovery tool that brings awareness and smarter habits bit by bit. Over time, this constant learning edge nudges you closer to financial independence.

For teens who want to take tracking a step further, some apps and spreadsheets let you plan ahead by creating budgets within the tool itself. Budgeting means deciding how much money you want to allocate for different categories like food, transportation, entertainment, and saving before the money is even spent. Then, tracking helps you see if you're sticking to those limits or need to adjust. This combination turns vague goals into concrete actions and real results.

It's normal to feel unsure about what method fits you best when you start. Try a few approaches and give each a week or two. Take notes on what feels easy, what feels like a hassle, and, most importantly, which system gives you useful info without stress. There's no one-size-fits-all answer, but the best choice is the one you will use regularly. This is the foundation for everything else in your financial journey, from budgeting to investing.

Whichever tools you use, the key is to make money-tracking a habit, not a one-time project. Imagine checking in every week, maybe Sunday evening, and updating your app, notes, or spreadsheet. This simple ritual builds a money habit you'll carry for life. Trust this process; it's not glamorous, but it's the engine behind smart spending, saving, and eventually investing. Financial freedom starts when you can clearly see and control your cash.

In the end, mastering money tracking at a young age turns what once felt stressful or confusing into a natural part of your daily routine. It gives you confidence and clarity to make decisions that align with your goals, rather than to random impulses or peer pressure. And as you get better at tracking, saving, and budgeting, you'll find it easier to free up money to invest early, the most powerful move you can make toward building wealth.

The steps are simple: choose your tool, dive in, and build the habit. Apps can automate and show instant insights. Notes sharpen awareness with each entry. Spreadsheets offer flexibility and control. It all leads to one result: you, in charge of your money, steadily building the foundation for a rich and independent future.

Final Thoughts

Starting your journey to wealth begins with knowing what you want, managing your money wisely, and having a safety net for the unexpected. Setting clear goals turns dreams into actionable steps, while a simple budget helps you control spending and prioritize savings. Even a small emergency fund can prevent stress and build confidence. Tracking your money regularly reveals spending habits, helps plug leaks, and keeps you on course toward your goals. By practicing these habits early, you create a strong foundation for financial independence and open the door to investing and long-term wealth.

Parents' Corner

Turn money talk into a fun mini-adventure. Ask your teen to show one recent purchase and guess if it was a need, want, or fun. Together, plan one small goal for the week, like saving a few coins or skipping a snack to add to fun money. Celebrate wins with high-fives or a silly reward. Keep it light, playful, and adventurous while building smart money habits.

Key Takeaways

- **Clarity Builds Direction:** Defining your financial goals transforms abstract dreams into specific, actionable plans. Whether it's saving for college, a car, or investing early, clarity gives purpose to every dollar you earn and spend.
- **Budgeting Provides Control:** Dividing money into needs, wants, and fun money gives you a structured way to manage finances. This approach prevents overspending and ensures that essential expenses are always covered while still allowing room for enjoyment.
- Emergency Funds Offer Security: Even a small safety net protects against unexpected expenses like phone repairs, transportation mishaps, or last-minute bills. Regular contributions to this fund build resilience and reduce financial stress.
- **Tracking Reveals Spending Habits:** Recording income and expenses exposes small, often-overlooked leaks, such as subscriptions or snacks. Reflection on these habits helps you

make intentional choices and redirect money toward goals that matter.

- **Early Habits Lead to Long-Term Wealth:** Developing routines around budgeting, saving, and tracking from a young age strengthens discipline and awareness. These habits form a foundation that carries forward into adult financial independence.
- **Alignment with Values Enhances Motivation:** Goals that reflect your personal values are easier to stick to. Money becomes a tool to pursue what truly matters, whether it's experiences, learning, or creative projects, rather than a source of stress or obligation.

📝 Dream Life Journal

Write about what your ideal life looks like by the time you turn 30. Describe where you want to live, what you want to own, and the experiences you hope to have. Then, think about the first small steps you can take now with your money to start moving toward that vision.

🎓Exercise: Tracking Your Money Habits

Take a week to observe and record how your money moves so you can understand your spending patterns and make smarter choices.

- Choose a week to carefully track every expense you make, no matter how small. Use a notebook, a phone app, or a spreadsheet to record each purchase. Include snacks, subscriptions, transportation, and even fun treats.
- At the end of the week, go through your records and categorize your spending into needs, wants, and fun money. Look for patterns and notice where most of your money went.
- Pay attention to the small, sneaky expenses—like coffee runs, in-app purchases, or online subscriptions—that quietly add up. Reflect on whether these purchases were necessary or if they could be reduced.
- Write a short paragraph about what surprised you the most. Did you spend more than you realized on wants? Did any habit stand out as something you could adjust?
- Based on your reflections, set one realistic goal for the next week. This could be saving a certain amount, limiting spending on a category, or redirecting money toward a bigger goal.
- Repeat this tracking process the following week and compare your results. Observe any improvements or changes in habits, and note how your awareness of money has grown.

This exercise encourages mindfulness about spending, helps identify wasteful habits, and reinforces the habit of tracking money as a step toward financial independence.

CHAPTER 3

Earn More Early: Part-Time Jobs, Side Hustles & Teen Income

> ***"Beware of little expenses; a small leak will sink a great ship."***
>
> **—Benjamin Franklin**

ONE OF THE smartest moves you can make when starting your journey to financial independence is to boost your income early by exploring part-time jobs, side hustles, and other teen-friendly earning opportunities that fit your schedule and skills. Whether it's turning your passion into cash, freelancing online, or grabbing a local gig, the key is to build habits that help you earn consistently while balancing school and your personal life. Earning early doesn't just mean more money now; it means more to invest, more experience to learn responsibility, and a mindset shift toward thinking like someone who creates wealth rather than just spends it.

By taking charge of how you bring in money, you lay the foundation for bigger financial moves down the road and build the confidence to ask for fair pay and negotiate raises without feeling awkward. Starting to earn now means time is working for you, and when paired with smart saving and investing, this combination turns teen income into serious wealth over the years.

Earning Options for Every Teen: Jobs, Gigs, and Online Work

Starting to earn money early is one of the smartest moves you can make to build wealth. Whether you want extra cash to invest, save for something big, or just have financial freedom, knowing where and how to earn is key. The good news? There's no shortage of options out there for teens, and they go way beyond the standard summer job or lawn mowing gig.

Traditional part-time jobs will probably be the first thing that comes to mind, right? Fast-food restaurants, retail stores, local libraries, and even movie theaters often hire teens for entry-level positions. These jobs aren't glamorous, but they come with consistent hours, a predictable paycheck, and opportunities to develop skills like customer service, time management, and teamwork—qualities that play well in any career or hustle down the line.

But if you're looking for ways to start earning without sticking to a fixed schedule, side gigs and freelance work may be a better fit. Thanks to the internet, even young people under 18 can find gigs that pay, sometimes well, based on their skills or availability. From dog walking, babysitting, and tutoring to helping neighbors with yard work or running errands, many gigs don't require a formal resume or a background check. They're flexible, allow you to be your own boss, and most importantly, you get to choose what kind of work suits you.

Online Gigs

Online work has exploded with opportunities, making it easier than ever for teens to earn without leaving their homes. Maybe you're good at writing, graphic design, coding, or social media. Platforms like Fiverr, Upwork, or even TikTok and YouTube provide spaces where teens can monetize their skills or create content that earns ad revenue or sponsorships. Some teens start websites or blogs, while others sell handmade crafts or digital products on Etsy or similar sites. The digital landscape opens a world of unrestricted earning opportunities, and it's a space most adults are still learning about.

But keep in mind, not every online opportunity is legit. It's important to spot red flags like gigs that ask for upfront payment or promise unrealistic returns for little work. Building a reputation and consistent income online takes time and effort, much like any other job.

Passion Projects and Internships

Another neat way to earn is by turning hobbies and interests into income streams. If you love photography, for example, selling pictures on stock photo sites or doing portraits for family and friends can get the ball rolling. Passion projects don't just fill up your free time; they can create real cash flow that sometimes outpaces traditional part-time paychecks.

Have you thought about internships or volunteer roles? While some don't pay, many programs geared toward teens offer stipends, and those stipends might lead to paid roles later. Plus, these positions build your resume with relevant experience and networking connections, both of which can open better earning doors in the future. Consider this a long-term investment in the same way you'd look at stocks or crypto. The payoff can come much later, but be far greater.

- **Part-Time Jobs:** Reliable, steady, and structured, like working in retail or food service.
- **Side Gigs:** Flexibility and variety, like pet sitting, tutoring, or lawn care.
- **Online Work:** Skills-focused and scalable, including freelance design, content creation, or website management.

Diving into paid opportunities early also teaches essential money skills—banking your income, managing taxes if you're freelancing, and figuring out how much to save versus spend. These lessons will serve you well when you begin investing. Remember, every dollar earned is a potential seed for your future wealth, especially when it's directed wisely.

☯️ Work-Life Balance

While earning money matters, balancing that with school and extracurriculars is a challenge. Taking on too much without planning can lead to burnout, which defeats the purpose of making extra cash. Start by setting realistic goals for how many hours a week you want to work, then experiment with different gigs or jobs to find what feels sustainable.

Some teens find success mixing part-time work during the school year with more intensive gigs or internships over the summer. That flexibility lets you keep your grades up while learning what earning paths resonate most. If your focus is on investing, even a small, consistent income can be funneled into building a seed fund to start with.

Negotiate Pay

Another overlooked but important angle is learning how to negotiate pay. For many jobs and gigs, your initial offer isn't final. As you gain confidence and demonstrate value, don't hesitate to ask for raises or better rates. This skill translates across life and is a must-have for maximizing earnings and investing capital over time.

At the core, there are plenty of options because the economy keeps evolving rapidly. What worked decades ago may not be the best fit now, and vice versa. A teen today can earn through traditional means, as well as through brand deals on social media, selling digital art NFTs, or managing small-business social accounts. Each route requires different investments in time and skill, but all share one thing in common: they start with your effort and grow from there.

📈 Document Your Earnings

Finally, regardless of which route you choose, it's important to document your earnings and keep track of what you're making. Open a bank account if you don't already have one, and build the habit of saving and budgeting as soon as the money hits your hand. You're laying the groundwork for a lifetime of financial health and investing success by treating your income seriously, even if the amounts seem small right now.

In a few years, the teen jobs and gigs you do today won't just be a memory. They'll be part of the foundation that lets you invest sooner, take smarter risks, and eventually step into true financial independence. So think of this as more than just finding ways to get cash; it's about building a mindset for wealth and opportunity that lasts your whole life.

Turning Skills & Hobbies into Side Hustles

If you've spent time developing skills or have hobbies that you're passionate about, turning those into side hustles can be one of the smartest ways to make money early on. Unlike traditional part-time jobs, side hustles let you leverage what you already enjoy or know how to do, which means work feels less like a chore and more like an opportunity. Plus, building something from your own skills gives you real-world experience that no classroom can teach, not to mention a great story for your resume or college applications down the road.

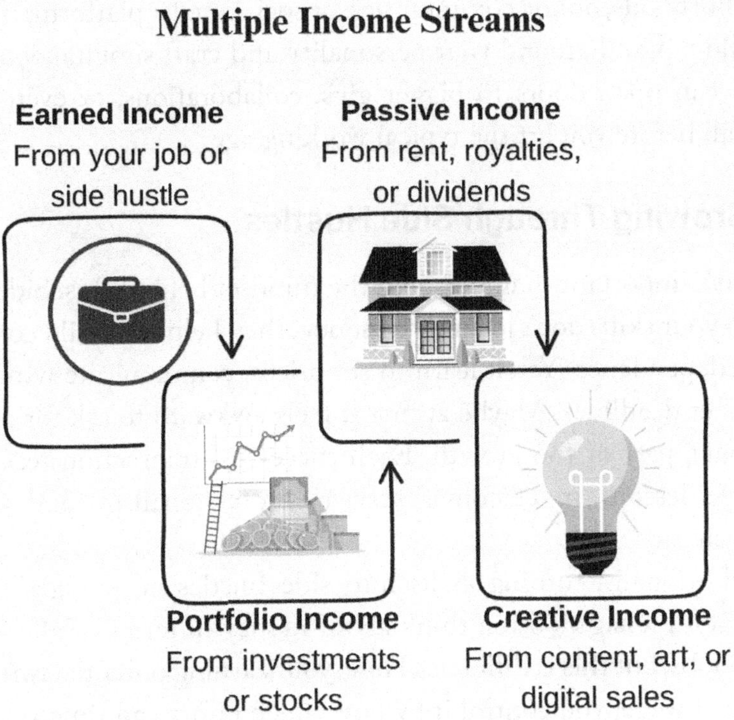

Recognize What Can Be Monetized

Think about it: do you have a knack for graphic design, can you play a musical instrument, or maybe you've mastered a sport or video editing? These aren't just "fun things" to pass the time. They're valuable talents that can be turned into income streams with a little creativity and effort. The key is recognizing that what you spend time practicing can be monetized, and often with low startup costs. For example, if you enjoy photography, you can start by offering photoshoots for birthdays or local events. Or if gaming is your passion, streaming your gameplay or coaching other players can generate money.

What makes side hustles connected to skills and hobbies even better is the potential to scale. Many teens start by doing small gigs for friends and family, but from there, they can expand their reach to local neighborhoods, online communities, or social media platforms. It's a way to build a brand around your personality and craft simultaneously. That brand can open doors to bigger gigs, collaborations, or even product sales, all before you hit the typical working age.

💻 Growing Through Side Hustles

Now, it's important to understand the mindset behind this. Side hustles tied to your skills don't just make money; they help you build confidence and independence. You'll learn to set prices, communicate with clients, and meet deadlines. Maybe at first it feels awkward to ask for payment, but that's part of the growth. Each successful transaction teaches you valuable lessons in customer service, professionalism, and financial responsibility.

Additionally, turning skills into side hustles encourages financial creativity. Teenagers often think about money in terms of allowance or hourly jobs, but this is different. Here, your earning potential isn't capped at a fixed wage; you control it by how much effort and time you put in. Want to earn more? Offer more services or increase your rates as you gain expertise. This freedom is empowering and crucial for developing an entrepreneurial mindset that will serve well beyond your teen years.

One of the challenges, though, is balancing quality with speed. Since it's your reputation on the line, it's better to deliver promising results than to rush and produce sloppy work. Over time, positive reviews and word of mouth become your best advertising. Managing client expectations and honing your craft simultaneously are crucial lessons that will make or break your side hustle. Remember, hobbies turned into income streams require professionalism, even if they started out as casual passions.

Creating Digital Presence

What about marketing your skills? Social media can be a powerful tool when it's used smartly. Creating Instagram or TikTok accounts dedicated to your work lets you showcase before-and-after photos, testimonials, tutorials, or your process. The authenticity that comes through when you create content about something you love resonates with people way more than a generic sales pitch. Plus, content doesn't have to be super polished; it just needs to be real and consistent.

Don't underestimate the power of community either. Local clubs, school groups, or online forums related to your hobby can be great places to connect with potential customers and collaborators. For example, if you're into graphic design, join a Discord server for creatives where people share jobs or opportunities. Or if you're talented at playing an instrument, performing at school events or family gatherings can get you referrals. It's all about putting yourself in spaces where your skills will be seen.

💰 Keeping Costs Low as You Build Your Hustle

Another important factor for this kind of side hustle is to keep your costs low as you get started. Using free or affordable tools and software helps keep your upfront investment minimal. For writers and editors, Google Docs or Grammarly can be enough to kick off a freelance editing gig. For artists and designers, apps like Canva and free drawing software can do the trick. Starting lean minimizes risk, meaning you don't have to worry about losing a big chunk of money if things don't take off immediately.

Being organized also matters. Keeping track of who you work for, how much they owe you, deadlines, and expenses can't be overlooked. Even simple spreadsheets work fine and help you understand cash flow right from the start. Learning to invoice professionally and follow up on payments sets you apart and prepares you for any work environment, whether it's freelance or full-time.

Remember, not all side hustles need to be directly tied to creative skills. Some teens thrive providing services like tutoring, dog walking, or house cleaning—activities that use their interpersonal and organizational skills. What counts is thinking critically about what you enjoy or excel at, and who might need that service. Turning hobbies into income doesn't always mean converting a talent into a product; sometimes, it's about solving problems or serving community needs.

Fun Fact

Side hustles create an extra layer of financial protection by giving you more control over how and when you earn. With additional income, you can save steadily or explore low-risk ways to grow your money without touching essential expenses. Building multiple income streams early increases flexibility and stability, supporting your long-term financial goals.

With dedication, a clear plan, and some hustle, what starts as a hobby can become a powerful stepping stone to financial independence. Don't be afraid to experiment, learn from mistakes, and keep improving your offerings. Turning skills and hobbies into side hustles isn't just about making money now; it's about setting the foundation for a lifetime of smart financial habits and personal growth.

How to Ask for a Raise or Better Pay Without Being Awkward

As a teen or young person dipping your toes into part-time jobs or side hustles, one of the most powerful skills you can develop is confidently asking for better pay. It might sound intimidating, but knowing how to ask for a raise or negotiate your rate without feeling awkward is crucial.

You're not just doing it to earn more now, but to set a strong foundation for your financial independence and future earning power.

First, realize that asking for a raise isn't about being pushy or entitled; it's about valuing your time, skills, and contributions. Employers expect conversations like this; it's a normal and healthy part of any working relationship. When you approach the topic thoughtfully, it becomes less about demands and more about collaboration. Your goal is to clearly and reasonably demonstrate your worth while keeping the conversation professional and positive.

Research and Prepare Thoroughly

Before you even bring up the subject, prepare. This isn't a casual chat; it's more like a mini presentation about why you deserve more. Dig into what you've actually done well in your role or gig. Have you taken on extra responsibilities, improved your skills, or gotten positive feedback? Maybe you've been reliable and consistent, or you went above and beyond in customer service. Write down specific examples. These aren't just talking points; they're proof that you've earned a raise.

Next, do your research. Find out what others in similar roles earn. This doesn't have to mean comparing yourself directly with coworkers; it can mean checking online job boards, talking to friends, or even asking industry professionals. Knowing the market rate helps you avoid lowballing yourself or asking for an amount that comes off as unrealistic. It also shows your employer that you're informed and serious about your work.

📞Select the Perfect Timing

Timing matters. Don't wait until your job performance reviews (if they exist); pick a moment when your employer is not rushed or stressed. Right after completing a big task or project, or after receiving positive feedback, can be ideal. Avoid peak busy times or moments of company chaos. A calm, positive environment means your request is more likely to be heard clearly.

When you're ready for the conversation, keep your tone confident but polite. You might say something like, "I really enjoy working here and want to keep growing with the team. Since I've taken on these extra tasks and consistently met my goals, I wanted to discuss the possibility of adjusting my pay to reflect that." This approach focuses on mutual benefit and progress, not just on what you want.

Be ready for questions or even a "no," and that's okay. Sometimes budgets are tight, or your employer needs more time to think. If they can't offer a raise right away, ask what steps you could take to work toward one in the future. This shows you're committed and open to feedback rather than just demanding more money. It might sound awkward, but it positions you as mature and forward-thinking.

Also, don't forget that negotiating pay isn't only about your hourly rate or salary. Sometimes there's room to negotiate perks like more flexible hours, extra breaks, or learning opportunities that can indirectly boost your value down the line. As a teen juggling school and work, better scheduling might be as valuable as more dollars. Always consider the total package.

Practice the Conversation

Practice helps. Role-playing your conversation with a friend, family member, or even in front of the mirror can boost your confidence and help smooth out any awkwardness. You don't have to memorize a script, but getting comfortable saying the key points aloud makes the real conversation easier and more natural. Remember, your delivery matters just as much as what you say.

One major mindset shift is to stop seeing asking for a raise as begging or confrontation. Instead, think of it as a professional conversation that benefits both sides. Employers want motivated, appreciated workers. When you show you understand your role's value and are willing to invest in yourself, it usually earns respect. Even if this is your first job or hustle, it's fine to be ambitious and expect fair pay.

Remember, early on, your goal is less about the exact dollar amount and more about building the habit and confidence to advocate for yourself. Every time you practice this skill, you build up a valuable muscle that will pay off massively as you move into internships, full-time jobs, or even your own business. Learning to communicate your worth clearly will help you unlock more opportunities and faster financial growth.

Log Your Wins

In addition, keep track of your wins and improvements over time. If your employer says "not yet" to a pay increase, consider setting up a check-in date a month or two later. Being proactive about following up makes you memorable and dedicated. It also proves you're serious about growth rather than just one-time requests.

Finally, don't let fear hold you back. The worst that can happen is they say no, or they need time to think. Neither outcome is a disaster. You're not risking your job by asking respectfully and professionally. And with every ask, you learn things that refine your negotiation next time. Approach this with curiosity instead of stress: What can I learn from this conversation? How can I improve my ask?

Fun Fact:
The average millionaire has seven streams of income, not just one!

So, to recap: prepare with facts and examples, research market pay, pick a good time, speak clearly and confidently, consider all parts of your compensation, and follow up if needed. Asking for a raise without awkwardness doesn't mean you have to be perfect; it means you show up ready, respectful, and focused on a win-win outcome. Do this regularly, and you'll be building not just your bank account, but a mindset that fuels long-term financial independence.

Parents' Corner

Create a fun, supportive environment where your teen can explore earning ideas with you.

How it works:

1. **Parents and teens each list 5 skills or hobbies** the teen has (separately).
2. Compare lists to see which skills both sides agree show the most potential.
3. Work together to design a **pretend mini-business** for one selected skill:
   - a simple logo (drawn or digital)
   - a catchy name
   - what the service/product is
   - who the customers might be
   - a sample pricing idea
4. End with a "pitch moment" where the teen presents their mini-business in a fun, low-pressure way.

Why it's valuable:

It strengthens communication, builds confidence, and helps parents understand their teen's interests—while giving the teen practice in entrepreneurship and self-expression.

Final Thoughts

Your part-time job or side hustle should amplify your growth, not drain your passion or health. Approaching your schedule with flexibility and awareness about your energy's ebb and flow can make all the difference between burning out and thriving. As you build smart money habits and invest early, remember that sustainable success depends on pacing yourself and protecting your most valuable resource: your well-being.

Balancing all this isn't easy, and it looks different for everyone. Some days might be more work-heavy, others more relaxed, and that's perfectly okay. What matters is maintaining a rhythm that lets you excel in your goals without sacrificing your health or happiness. By cultivating this balance now, you set a foundation for greater success—financial and personal—as you grow into adulthood.

Key Takeaways

- **Early Earning Builds Long-Term Wealth:** Starting to earn while you're young gives you a head start on saving, investing, and building financial confidence. Even small early earnings compound into big opportunities later in life when managed well.
- **Teens Have More Earning Options Than Ever Before:** From traditional part-time jobs to flexible gigs and online freelance work, teens can earn in ways that match their personal interests, schedule, and skills—including passions like art, photography, gaming, or music.
- **Side Hustles Turn Hobbies Into Income:** Skills you already practice—graphic design, tutoring, sports, writing, editing, crafts, or video creation—can become profitable side hustles. These also build experience, professionalism, and a portfolio you can grow over time.
- **Negotiating Pay Is a Skill, Not a Confrontation:** Learning how to ask for a raise or adjust your rates teaches self-advocacy, communication, and confidence. Preparation, timing, and understanding your worth are key to asking without awkwardness.

- **Work-Life-School Balance Protects Your Energy:** Your schedule should support your goals—not exhaust you. Sleep, planning, boundaries, nutrition, and downtime all help maintain the energy you need to thrive at work, school, and in life.

📝 Dream Life Journal

"If money, time, and fear were not barriers, what kind of job, side hustle, or passion-based business would I start today—and why?"

Reflect on what excites you, what skills you want to grow, and how this vision connects to your future financial independence.

🎓 Exercise: Energy Budget Audit

Use this page to understand when your energy is highest and lowest throughout the week.

1. Track Your Energy Levels Throughout the Week

(Write what time you felt energized or tired each day)

Day 1: Energized: ____________________ Tired: ____________________

Day 2: Energized: ____________________ Tired: ____________________

Day 3: Energized: ____________________ Tired: ____________________

Day 4: Energized: ____________________ Tired: ____________________

Day 5: Energized: ____________________ Tired: ____________________

Day 6: Energized: ____________________ Tired: ____________________

Day 7: Energized: ____________________ Tired: ____________________

2. Which Activities Drained Your Energy?

____

____

____

____

3. Which Activities Re-Energized You?

____

____

____

____

4. Two Adjustments You Can Make for Better Balance:

Adjustment 1: ____

Adjustment 2: ____

CHAPTER 4

Saving on Autopilot: Paying Your Future Self First

> ***The philosophy of the rich and the poor is this: the rich invest their money and spend what is left. The poor spend their money and invest what is left."***
>
> **– Robert Kiyosaki**

ONE OF THE smartest moves you can make when building wealth is to pay your future self before anyone else gets a cut, and the easiest way to do this is by automating your savings. It's simple: as soon as you get money, whether from a job, allowance, or side hustle, set up automatic transfers to move a portion into your savings or investment account without having to think twice. This "pay yourself first" approach turns saving from a chore into a seamless habit that runs in the background, so you avoid the temptation to spend what you haven't yet seen. Over time, those small, consistent amounts add up, giving your money more time to grow and work for you.

By creating this autopilot system early, you're not just saving; you're respecting your future goals, reducing financial stress, and setting yourself up for financial independence long before most people even start thinking about it.

The "Pay Yourself First" Rule Explained

One of the simplest yet most powerful habits you can develop early on is the "Pay Yourself First" rule. It's a money mindset shift that changes how you view saving and spending. Instead of waiting until the end of the month (or worse, the last paycheck) to see what's left over, you treat your savings like a bill that has to be paid every single time you get money. Imagine paying your future self first before anyone else—before bills, before video games, or that new pair of sneakers. That's precisely how you start building wealth automatically.

The magic here is in the word "first." When you prioritize your future self over current temptations, you're using your money to build freedom and opportunities down the road.

Start small, stay consistent, even tiny savings can snowball into wealth

Why Paying Yourself First Builds Real Wealth

Because money habits are often the biggest obstacle to financial success, most people think saving is something to do if they have time or extra cash. But those few people who get rich and stay rich aren't better luckers; they have learned to pay themselves first consistently, turning saving into an automatic system. This prevents the common "I'll save later" trap, where saving is always delayed, and spending always wins in the moment.

You don't need a lot to get started, either. Even saving a small chunk, like 5% or 10% of any money you get, can explode over time thanks to compound interest. This means your money doesn't just sit there; it grows, earning returns that then earn returns of their own. Starting early, while you're still young, means your savings have more time to grow, making your future self thank you over and over.

⚖️ Balance Your Priorities

Some people worry that if they pay themselves first, they won't have enough left to enjoy life or cover necessary expenses. That's part of the reason why it's essential to set a realistic percentage that fits your current income and life situation. It's not about sacrificing all fun or essentials, but about balancing your priorities. You want to build a habit that's easy to keep, not something so harsh you give up after a week.

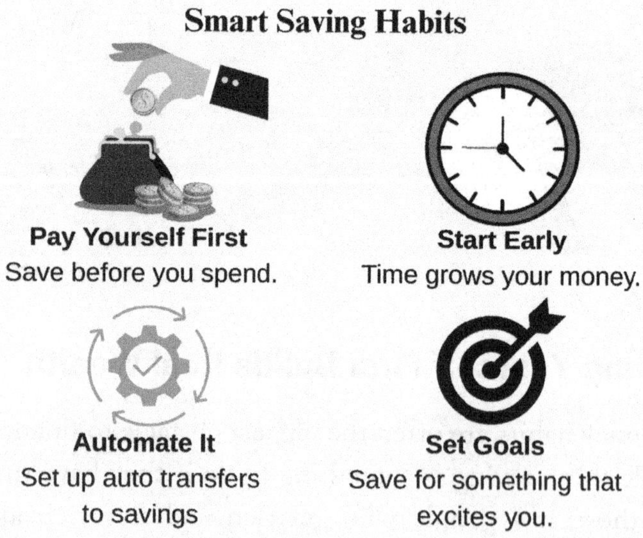

Plus, the beauty of the pay-yourself-first rule is that it aligns perfectly with automatic savings. Once you decide on an amount or percentage, you can automate transfers from your checking to your savings or investment accounts. This hands-off method means you don't have to remember or even think about it after setup. Your money moves quietly and consistently toward your future goals, while you focus on other things like school, hobbies, or crushing that side hustle.

Mental Clarity and Discipline

Another reason the pay-yourself-first rule is so powerful is that it simplifies decision-making. When saving is automatic and upfront, you don't have to wrestle with "should I save or should I spend?" each time cash comes in. This mental clarity reduces financial stress and guilt, freeing you to make smarter spending choices with what's left. Instead of debating whether to save this month or blow it all on the latest drop of sneakers or concert tickets, you've already decided: saving comes first, always.

It also teaches discipline—a skill that pays off in all areas of life. Discipline around money is like exercising a muscle. The more you practice paying yourself first, the easier it becomes to manage bigger financial responsibilities down the road. And when emergencies hit or big opportunities come up, you'll have the practice and resources to handle them without panic.

Choose a Fixed Percentage

Some teens worry that because they earn irregular income, maybe through gig work, family chores, or seasonal jobs, the rule is hard to apply. But that's precisely when *Pay Yourself First* can shine. Instead of saving uneven amounts or nothing at all, you can choose a percentage to set aside whenever you get paid. This method actually smooths out the ups and downs of irregular earnings and helps maintain steady progress.

Lastly, paying yourself first connects your present choices with your future dreams. It's easy to say, "I want to have a house someday," or "I want to travel the world." But those dreams won't just fall into your lap. By consistently putting money aside, even before you enjoy other things, you're turning dreams into goals and goals into reality. It's a daily demonstration of valuing your future self as much as, or more than, your present desires.

Imagine hundreds or thousands of dollars sitting in an account that's working for you, growing through investments, while you focus on school or hobbies. That's what "pay yourself first" sets into motion, a lifelong habit that builds your wealth quietly but steadily. It isn't flashy or complicated, but it's one of the smartest moves anyone, especially young people, can make. Starting this rule early can mean the difference between struggling financially in your twenties and having the freedom to choose your path without money holding you back.

So, the next time money comes your way, remind yourself that paying yourself first isn't just a rule; it's a way of respecting your future and making sure it's bright. It's a financial superpower that anyone can start, no matter how small their income, and it's the foundation for everything that comes next in your journey toward wealth.

Fun Fact

Apps like Acorns and Chime can automatically round up your purchases to the nearest dollar and save the extra change, helping your savings grow effortlessly.

Making Saving Fun: Challenges, Rewards, and Visual Trackers

Saving money can sometimes feel like a drag, especially when it's money you don't get to spend right now. But what if saving felt less like a chore and more like a game you actually wanted to play? Turning saving into something fun makes it way easier to stick with, even when the temptation to spend pops up. Instead of seeing saving as boring, you start treating it like a personal challenge, with rewards and progress you can actually see. That's the secret to making the "pay yourself first" rule more than just a rule; it becomes part of your lifestyle.

Set a Challenge

One of the best ways to make saving enjoyable is to set challenges for yourself. These might sound simple, but they work because they add a sense of excitement and achievement. For example, challenge yourself to save a certain amount each week or month. It could be $5, $10, or even just $1, depending on what feels doable. The key is the consistent effort, not the size of the amount. Every time you hit your goal, you're proving to yourself that saving is possible and rewarding. Over time, these small wins build serious momentum.

Challenges don't always have to be solo. If you've got siblings, friends, or even an online community, try turning it into a group challenge. Imagine a friendly competition where each of you shares progress, cheers each other on, and compares savings growth. This social element boosts motivation; it's hard to slack off when you know others are keeping track and rooting for you. Plus, it's cool to talk about money goals without stress or judgment when you're all in the same boat.

🌱 Reward Yourself

Rewarding yourself is equally important when saving. It sounds counterintuitive to spend money while trying to save, but rewards help keep your motivation high. The trick is to pick rewards that don't kill your progress, maybe small treats that make saving feel worthwhile. Say you set aside $50 this month without breaking it, and then let yourself buy that new pair of headphones or enjoy a fun outing. It's about celebrating milestones and acknowledging your effort, so saving never feels like giving up something important.

Use Visual Trackers

Visual trackers make savings feel real. Looking at numbers in a bank account alone can feel abstract, especially when you're just starting. But charts, graphs, or even a simple progress bar you color in on a poster can turn your goal into something tangible. When you see your savings growing day by day or week by week, it's harder to ignore the progress or give up. This visual reinforcement builds a positive feedback loop: the more you see yourself doing well, the more you want to keep going.

You might be surprised at what a colorful savings jar or digital tracker can do. Some teens even use apps that round up their everyday purchases and automatically deposit the spare change into a savings account. Watching your balance increase this way feels effortless and satisfying, almost like a game where you earn points without noticing. This "set it and forget it" style supports the pay-yourself-first mindset and removes the temptation to spend that extra change.

Another way to make visual tracking more enjoyable is to link your savings progress to your long-term dreams. If you're aiming to invest in stocks, start your own business, or travel by the time you're 21, create a chart that shows exactly how close you are to funding those goals. For instance, if your goal is $1,000 for your first investment account, break it down into chunks and celebrate each milestone. The more personal and vivid your goal feels, the more driven you'll be to save without fail.

🤔 Try Creative Ideas

Beyond just tracking, try mixing up your challenges with creative ideas like "no spend" days or weeks. For example, challenge yourself to go seven days without buying anything non-essential, then put that saved money straight into your savings. It's a double win; you train yourself to resist impulse spending and build your savings faster than expected. Some teens even pair this with journaling about how they felt during the challenge, which helps build awareness around their habits.

Rewards don't always need to be about stuff, either. Consider setting non-material prizes, such as a day off from chores, a special outing with friends, or time dedicated to an activity you love. These intangible rewards give your brain a hit of positive reinforcement without risking undoing your financial progress. It's a smart way to stay motivated because not every reward needs cash to feel satisfying.

The Ability to Reset

It's easy to fall off track with saving, especially when school, friends, or hobbies take up all your attention. That's where visual trackers shine again. When you can see exactly how much you saved last month versus this month, it's a reminder that even small dips don't erase past effort. You can always reset or tweak your goals, and having that visual record helps you bounce back faster without feeling like you failed.

Games and apps designed specifically for money-saving can also turn financial goals into a source of fun. Some will let you earn badges, unlock achievements, or even compete in leaderboards for hitting savings benchmarks. This taps into the natural human love for earning rewards and recognition — the same reason video games are so addictive. The better you get at the "game" of saving, the more motivated you become to win, and that's a mindset shift worth chasing.

⭐ Visual Reminders

Creating visual reminders around you also helps, like post-it notes on your mirror or phone wallpaper of your goals. When you see those every day, saving becomes a little habit that creeps into your brain without effort. It's a low-key but effective nudge that helps you prioritize your future self. Plus, it makes the whole process less abstract and way more personal.

One simple trick is to set your savings goal to be competitive with your past months' savings. Instead of stressing over hitting a fixed number, aim to save just a little more than last time. This method feels manageable and less overwhelming while tapping into the power of daily or weekly progress. You get the thrill of growth without pressure to be perfect, and that's what builds long-term consistency.

Align Your Challenges with Your Values

At this age, it's also helpful to tie your savings challenges and rewards to your interests. If you love tech, maybe your challenge is saving enough for your first smart gadget. If you're into fashion, tie savings to a piece you want but don't buy impulsively. When your goals reflect what genuinely excites you, saving stops feeling like a sacrifice and becomes a path toward something you really want.

Finally, remember that saving isn't just about money piling up; it's about creating habits that shape your future freedom. When fun elements like challenges, rewards, and visual trackers become part of your money routine, they help you build a mindset that sticks. You're not just putting dollars away; you're training yourself for smart, intentional decisions that'll pay off big down the road. And, trust me, once saving starts to feel like a game you actually want to win, there's no limit to what you can achieve.

Fun Fact:
If you save just $5 a day, you'll have over $1,800 in a year and even more if it earns interest!

What To Do When You Fall Off Track Without Giving Up

Let's face it: saving on autopilot isn't always seamless. Life happens—maybe you miss a few automatic transfers to your savings account, or some unexpected expenses pop up that drain your funds. Falling off track is less about failure and more about everyday moments that everyone experiences on their journey toward financial independence. The key isn't messing up; it's what you do after you slip that counts. Here are a few strategies:

- **Don't Be Hard on Yourself:** Missing a deposit or falling behind doesn't mean failure. Many people feel frustrated when they slip up, but saving and investing is a long-term game. Treat setbacks as resets, not disasters. Consistency over time is far more powerful than aiming for perfection. Showing up regularly, even imperfectly, builds momentum and strengthens your financial habits.
- **Pause and Reflect:** When you notice you've fallen off track, take a moment to understand why. Did an unexpected expense come up? Are your goals unrealistic for your current income? Did your automatic transfers stop working? Identifying the cause helps

you find practical solutions, like adjusting spending habits or temporarily saving smaller amounts until you can return to your intended plan.

- **Take Action Quickly:** The longer you wait to get back on track, the harder it becomes. Even small steps, like saving $5 or $10, are better than doing nothing. Restarting your habit matters more than the amount you save initially. Remember, the "pay yourself first" principle isn't about hitting huge targets immediately—it's about prioritizing saving each time you get paid.
- **Track and Motivate Yourself:** Create a system to stay motivated and accountable. Visual tracking—through apps, charts, or notebooks—helps you see progress over time. Watching even small increases in your savings can be a huge confidence boost. Rewarding yourself occasionally for reaching milestones makes the process feel enjoyable and reinforces good habits.
- **Understand Setbacks Are Normal:** Missing a week of saving or dipping into your emergency fund doesn't erase your past progress. Think of money habits like muscles: they strengthen with consistent effort, even if sometimes you're a little inconsistent. Setbacks are part of the journey, and learning to recover gracefully builds long-term resilience.
- **Revisit Your "Why":** When you feel tempted to give up, remind yourself why you started saving and investing. Maybe it's to buy a car, move out on your own, or achieve financial freedom by your 30s. Keeping your goals visible—on your desk, phone, or wall—provides daily nudges to stay focused and motivated through challenging moments.

Fun Fact

Over 75% of people use a budget to reach their financial goals, and even small amounts saved through budgeting can help build financial independence over time.

It's also okay to adjust your plan. Life isn't static, and neither are your income or expenses. Maybe your first budget or savings goal was too aggressive, and you ended up burning out quickly. That's a cue to tweak things, not to throw the whole plan out. Flexible goals that grow with you keep the process sustainable instead of overwhelming.

Don't hesitate to ask for help or advice. Whether it's a financially savvy friend, a family member, or even a teacher, talking through your challenges can spark new ideas or encouragement you didn't see before. Sometimes, just knowing someone else has been through the same ups and downs makes sticking to your goals feel more doable.

One last piece of advice: practice patience. Compound interest and wealth-building don't explode overnight; they simmer and grow slowly. Missing a month or two of saving won't destroy your future potential, but giving up entirely will. Keep going, keep adjusting, and trust the process. Real financial independence comes not from perfection but from persistence.

To sum up, falling off track happens to everyone, especially when you're just starting. Instead of quitting, analyze what went wrong, reset your expectations, restart your habits, and lean on automations and motivation tools. Believe in the power of small, regular actions, even if they're imperfect. As long as you keep paying yourself first, your future self will end up with the reward.

Final Thoughts

This chapter shows that one of the smartest ways to build wealth early is by prioritizing yourself, paying your future self first. Automating savings through transfers or round-up apps turns saving from a chore into a seamless habit, letting your money grow quietly over time. Even small percentages, saved consistently, benefit from compounding and set the stage for long-term financial independence.

The "pay yourself first" rule isn't about perfection; it's about consistency, discipline, and connecting daily choices to your future goals.

Using visual trackers, challenges, and small rewards can make saving fun, motivating, and tangible, turning a financial routine into a game you want to win.

Setbacks are normal, but reflecting, adjusting, and restarting quickly ensures progress continues. By staying flexible, tracking your wins, and keeping your "why" in mind, you build habits that strengthen over time. With patience, persistence, and automation, paying yourself first becomes a powerful foundation for financial freedom and a lifetime of smart money habits.

Parents' Corner

Invite your teen to walk through a simple "Pay Yourself First" routine together. Start by having them choose a small percentage of any money they receive—whether from chores, a job, or gifts—and discuss how that amount could grow over time. Sit down with them to set up an automatic transfer (or a mock version if they don't have their own account yet) so they can see how saving can happen quietly in the background.

Key Takeaways

- **Pay Yourself First:** Treat saving as a non-negotiable priority by setting aside money for your future before spending on anything else.
- **Automate Savings:** Automatic transfers remove the temptation to spend first and make saving a consistent habit.
- **Small Amounts Grow:** Even modest, regular savings grow significantly over time thanks to compound interest.
- **Balance is Important:** Choose a realistic percentage to save so you can enjoy life while still investing in your future.
- **Set Up Visual Motivation:** Tracking progress visually helps reinforce habits and makes savings feel tangible and rewarding.

- **Consistency Over Perfection:** Occasional slip-ups are normal; what matters is restarting and maintaining the habit over the long term.

Dream Life Journal

Imagine your life five years from now. Write about what you hope to have achieved financially, what your daily life looks like, and how paying yourself first now could help make those dreams a reality. Then, list one small action you can take this week to start building that future."

🎓 Exercise: "Savings Challenge Tracker"

Turn saving into a game! Pick a small amount of money to save each week—$1, $5, or $10, depending on what feels doable. Each time you save, color in a box on the tracker below. Set mini-rewards for milestones to celebrate your progress and keep the game exciting. Challenge yourself to save a little more than last week or try a "no-spend" day to boost your savings even faster.

Your Savings Challenge Tracker

Week	Amount Saved	Boxes to Color	Reward
1			
2			
3			
4			
5			
6			
7			
8			

CHAPTER 5

Investing 101: How Wealth Actually Grows

"Success is walking from failure to failure with no loss of enthusiasm."

– Winston Churchill

INVESTING ISN'T ABOUT quick wins or guessing which stock will explode overnight; it's the steady process of putting your money to work so it grows over time, even while you sleep. When you invest, you're essentially buying a small piece of a company or lending your money in a way that can earn you returns, which, when combined with time, have the power to multiply into real wealth. The magic happens through compound growth, where the profits you make start earning their own profits, creating a snowball effect that smooths out ups and downs as markets fluctuate.

While there's risk involved, it's not a guaranteed paycheck. The longer you stay invested and the smarter your investment mix, the more you can reduce that risk and watch your money grow faster than if it just sat in a savings account. This chapter lays the foundation for understanding the mechanics of investing, so you can make confident decisions and begin building a portfolio that aligns with your goals and timeline.

What Investing Really Is and Isn't

Investing often gets put on a pedestal, talked about like some magical thing that only grown-ups with fancy job titles or tons of money can do. But the truth is, investing is really just a tool, a way to put your money to work so it can grow over time. It isn't gambling, a get-rich-quick scheme, or something that requires a secret formula. Instead, investing is about patience, planning, and understanding risk. Getting this clear from the start will save you a lot of frustration and help you build real wealth early on.

First off, investing isn't about making fast cash. If you're imagining flashing lights, wild bets, or instantly doubling your money, you're thinking more along the lines of gambling or day trading. Those activities might seem exciting, but they are dangerous, especially for beginners. Investing involves smart decisions over years, sometimes decades, allowing your money to grow steadily. The most potent force behind investing? Time and patience.

What Is Investing?

Investing means using your money to **buy a small piece of something** you think will be worth **more later**.

For example:

- When you buy a stock, you own a tiny piece of a company.
- When you buy a bond, you are loaning money to a company or the government, and they pay you back extra money as a "thank you."
- Some people invest in houses, buildings, or digital money because they hope those things **grow** in value over time.

The goal is to let your money grow, instead of just sitting still.

Saving vs. Investing

Saving and investing are not the same.

- Saving means putting money in a safe place, like a piggy bank or a bank account.
- Saving is good, but the money usually doesn't grow much.

There's a problem, though: over time, things cost more (like snacks, toys, and games). This is called inflation. That means your saved money can slowly buy less than before. Investing helps your money grow faster, so it can keep up with rising prices.

Is Investing Risky?

Yes, investing has **risk**, which means your money can sometimes go down before it goes up.

This can happen because:

- A company has a bad year
- The economy changes
- Big world events happen

That sounds scary, but investing is not gambling. Gambling is just guessing. Investing is making smart choices by learning, planning, and being patient.

🎯 Taking Smart Risks

Some people think the safest thing is to hide money or never invest it. But that can actually be risky too, because inflation slowly makes money weaker. Taking small, smart risks helps your money grow over time. That's how people build wealth and reach big goals. In short, saving keeps your money safe, but investing helps your money grow.

🕒 Time Makes Early Investing Powerful

Some people think investing is really hard or only for experts who know lots of big money words. But the basics are actually simple, and you don't need to be a finance expert to start. What matters most is being patient, building good habits, and remembering that investing is a long race, not a quick sprint. Easy choices, like putting your money into funds that spread it across many different companies, can work really well and don't take much effort.

Another myth is that investing means constant monitoring and instant decisions. Actually, one of the biggest benefits of investing is that you can set it and mostly forget it. Think of it like planting that tree again—you water it and check in occasionally, but you don't uproot it every week. By staying invested and resisting the urge to panic-sell or chase the latest trend, you harness the full power of your money's growth potential.

In fact, many experts agree that your biggest advantage as a young investor is time. The earlier you start, the more you can let compounding work. This means investing now, even if it feels like a tiny amount or if you're still figuring out your budget. Waiting to invest "until you know more" or "have more money" often means missing out on years of growth. So don't wait until everything is perfect; start today with what you have.

Smart Investing in 4 Steps

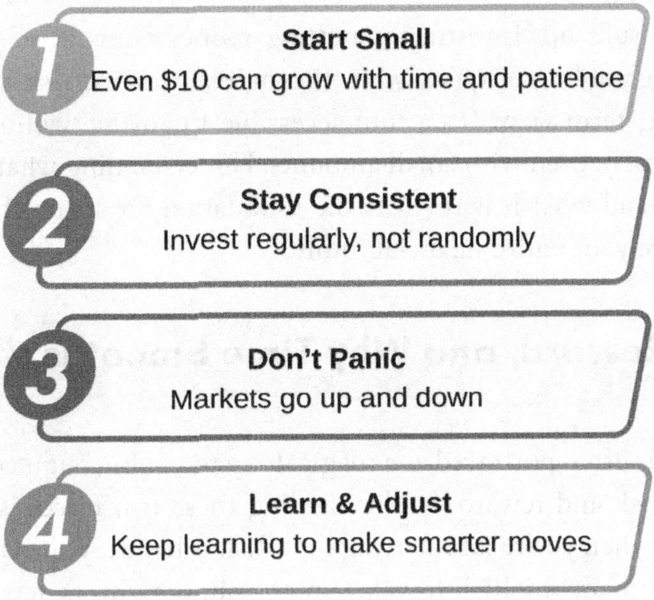

It's also important to realize that investing isn't about getting rich overnight or covering short-term needs. If you have money coming in that you might need soon—for a trip, a phone upgrade, or school supplies—that money should stay safe in savings. Investing is for money you won't touch for years. When you accept this timeline, you avoid panic when markets go down and give your money a chance to grow unhindered by quick wants.

Investing Builds Lasting Freedom

Finally, investing isn't complicated when you have the right mindset and knowledge. It boils down to making steady, informed choices, learning to ride out ups and downs, and allowing your money to grow over many years. Mistakes will happen, but that's part of learning. The key is to start, keep it simple, and build good habits that serve you for life. Smart investing unlocks financial freedom, letting you focus on what really matters, whether that's college, starting a business, or living the life you dream of.

So, to sum up: Investing is putting money to work to grow over time, not gambling or quick wins. It requires patience, risk acceptance, and a long-term view. It's a tool accessible to anyone willing to learn and start early, even with small amounts. Understanding what investing really is—and what it isn't—sets the foundation for smart choices that can change your entire financial future.

Risk, Reward, and Why Time Smooths the Ride

Investing is often portrayed as a magical key to wealth, but it comes with a mix of risk and reward. Understanding these two forces is essential, especially when you're just starting out. Risk is basically the chance that your investment might lose value in the short term. A reward is the potential gain you get for taking that risk. It's kind of like a game where you have to decide how much you're willing to bet in hopes of winning bigger prizes.

For young investors like you, risk isn't something to fear completely; it's something to manage thoughtfully. The single biggest advantage you have is time. When you start investing early, you have years, even decades, of time to let your money grow and recover from the ups and downs of the market. That's what "time smoothing the ride" really means. Markets are never perfectly steady; they go up and down like a roller coaster. But over long periods, those ups and downs tend to even out, making risk less scary than it seems at first glance.

The idea of risk might sound intimidating; after all, no one wants to watch their money shrink. However, the risk you face when investing is closely linked to the rewards you can expect over time. If you play it too safe, say by leaving your money in a basic savings account, it might be secure, but it won't grow much beyond a little interest. On the other hand, investing in stocks or other volatile assets could lead to greater growth. That extra reward comes with some bumps along the way.

Why You Should Invest

You might wonder why someone your age should invest when the market can suddenly drop or stocks can lose value fast. The big reason is time. When you start early, your money has lots of years to grow and recover from bumps along the way. Even if the market goes down sometimes, it usually has time to bounce back.

Another powerful idea is called compound growth, which means your money earns money, and then that money earns even more money. If you start investing at 13 or 18, you could have 50 years or more before you're older, giving your investments a long time to grow. With that much time, small losses don't matter as much, and your money has a better chance to grow into something big.

Understanding Risk Helps Your Money Grow Smarter

One important thing to remember is that risk isn't just about losing money; it's about the chance that your money won't grow as much as you hoped. For teenagers, that could mean saving less for your future vacations, college, or even your first house. The bigger the risk, the bigger the swings in your portfolio's value. And those swings can tempt you to make emotional decisions, like selling during a dip, which usually leads to locking in losses. Time helps smooth those emotional and financial bumps, so you can stay invested and actually reap the rewards.

Another way to think about risk is to look at how different investments can be more or less risky. Stocks are riskier because their prices can go up and down quickly if something happens with the company or the economy. Bonds are usually safer because they are like loans—you give your money to a company or the government, and they pay it back with a little extra money called interest. Cryptocurrency can be super unpredictable, like a wild roller coaster, and comes with its own special risks.

Because the future is uncertain, no one can predict exactly how an investment will perform. But history shows that, over the long term, taking some smart risks is usually worth it. Those who put all their money in super safe places often miss out on the higher returns that come with more adventurous investing. And when you're starting young, that difference really adds up.

Diversify Your Investments

To make the most of this, you don't have to pick every winning stock or time the market perfectly. Instead, spreading your investments across lots of different things, like stocks in various companies, bonds, and maybe some real estate funds, helps manage risk. This is called diversification. It's like not putting all your eggs in one basket, so if one investment doesn't do well, others can help carry the load.

When you combine diversification with a long time horizon, you create a powerful recipe for growing wealth. Say you put money into a stock index fund that tracks the overall market. The market will go up and down, but over decades, it has generally increased in value because economies grow, companies innovate, and people keep buying products and services. Time helps you ride out any temporary problems and gives your gains a chance to grow.

On the flip side, if you never take any risk, your money grows slowly, sometimes barely outpacing inflation. Inflation is what makes things cost more over time, so if your money isn't growing faster than inflation, it's really losing purchasing power. That's a hidden risk: the risk that your money won't keep up with the world around you.

It's important to feel a bit uneasy sometimes about risk because it means you're paying attention. You should understand that investing isn't a sure thing, but also recognize that doing nothing or playing it too safe can quietly erode your future wealth. For young investors, the challenge is not avoiding risk altogether but learning how much risk feels comfortable and how to stay consistent as time does its magic.

Fun Fact

The first stock exchange was established in Amsterdam in 1602 by the Dutch East India Company.

Time Is Your Go-To Strategy

So how does time actually smooth the ride? It's because short-term volatility—those sudden ups and downs—has less impact on your investments as the years go by. The longer you stay invested, the more likely it is that your average returns will reflect the overall growth of the economy and businesses. That's why time is your go-to strategy for surviving market downturns and coming out ahead.

When people talk about investing, they often focus on finding the secret "best stock" or the next hot cryptocurrency. While those things can be exciting, the real secret to wealth is simply staying invested and letting time do the heavy lifting. Patience and consistency beat chasing after quick wins every single time.

To put it simply, if you're starting to invest in your teens or early twenties, don't freak out over every market crash. Instead, think in decades. If one year or two don't go as planned, it's okay because time will give your investments a chance to recover. That long-term view is what separates successful investors from those who give up too soon.

In the end, risk and reward are two sides of the same coin, and the longer you give your money to work for you, the more time you have to smooth out the rough patches. The earlier you understand this, the easier it will be to build a strong foundation for lasting wealth.

Key Concepts: Diversification, Inflation, and Liquidity

Once you've got a handle on what investing is and the basics of risk and reward, there are a few important ideas you need to fully understand so your money can actually grow and stay safe over time. Those three foundations are diversification, inflation, and liquidity. Each plays a crucial role in how your investments behave and how much wealth you'll build in the long run. Let's break them down and see why they matter so much.

Diversification

It is the idea of not putting all your eggs in one basket. It sounds simple, but so many beginning investors overlook it or misunderstand it completely. When you diversify, you spread your money across different types of investments, such as stocks. This way, if one part of your portfolio tanks, the rest might hold steady or even grow. Without diversification, you become vulnerable to large losses if a single investment or sector fails.

Think about investing as if you're assembling a team for a group project at school. If you pick only one friend who's great at math but struggles with writing or research, your project might suffer in other areas. But if you have teammates who bring diverse skills to the table, your overall project is more likely to succeed. Diversification works the same way with money. By combining investments that react differently to the market, you reduce the risk your portfolio faces. Some investments might soar when the economy is doing well, while others might actually do better during slowdowns.

This doesn't mean you need to own hundreds of stocks to diversify. In fact, owning too many investments can get complicated fast and make it tough to manage your money. The goal is to find the right balance, which usually means a mix of a few broad investments, like index funds or ETFs, that already include many companies inside them. These funds automatically provide diversification for small investors who can't buy hundreds of individual shares.

Inflation

Another important idea for investors to understand is inflation. Inflation means that prices for things like food, clothes, and games slowly go up over time, so your money doesn't buy as much as it used to. For example, a candy bar that costs $1 today might cost $1.10 next year. That extra 10 cents seems small, but over many years, inflation can really add up. If your money just sits in a piggy bank or a regular savings account, inflation slowly makes it worth less.

Inflation: The Shark Tax

WITH TIME, PAY MORE FOR LESS

Investing is one way to fight inflation and help grow your money's value over time. Certain types of investments, especially stocks, can grow faster than inflation and increase your purchasing power. But some assets don't keep up; they might seem stable, but actually lose ground when inflation is high, like traditional savings accounts or cash kept under your mattress. Knowing about inflation helps you choose where to put your money so it actually grows instead of shrinking in real terms.

Most people overlook inflation because price increases are usually small and gradual. However, even a 2% inflation rate means the value of your money drops about 20% over ten years. That's why just saving is often not enough to build wealth. Your investments need to grow at least as much as inflation, ideally faster, to increase your real net worth. This is why understanding inflation changes how you think about risk and reward in investing. Higher expected returns usually come with higher risk, but aiming to beat inflation is key to preserving your money's future value.

Liquidity

Liquidity is just a word that means how easy it is to turn something into money. Some things, like stocks or digital money, are easy to sell fast, like in a few clicks on an app. Other things, like houses or rare toys, take a long time to sell and can cost extra money to do it. The easier something is to turn into cash, the more "liquid" it is.

Liquidity is important because sometimes you need your money fast, like for emergencies or a sudden opportunity. If your money is tied up in things that take a long time to sell, you might be stuck when you really need it. On the other hand, things that are easy to sell, like stocks, can change in price a lot and might not grow as steadily. So, finding the right mix of easy-to-sell and harder-to-sell investments is smart.

For long-term investing, having some less liquid things, like bonds or real estate, can be good because they often give steady income and don't jump up and down in price as much. But you should also keep some money in cash or very liquid investments so you don't have to sell other investments at a bad time.

A common tip is to have an emergency fund in cash, then invest the rest in a mix of easy-to-sell and less liquid things. This way, you're ready for surprises without missing out on money growth. Liquidity isn't just for convenience; it helps your money be flexible and safe when life throws curveballs.

Putting It All Together

Understanding these three concepts—diversification, inflation, and liquidity—gives you a powerful framework to make smart investing choices. Diversification helps you protect your portfolio from big losses, inflation reminds you why simply saving isn't enough, and liquidity ensures you have access to funds when needed without unnecessary losses.

Remember, investing isn't about quick wins or chasing the latest trends. It's about building a solid foundation that steadily and safely grows your wealth for your future. By applying these ideas as you start your investing journey, you're setting yourself up to make your money work harder and smarter. That's the real secret behind how wealth actually grows.

Keeping an eye on these key concepts will also make other parts of investing less scary. When you learn about stocks, bonds, or crypto in the next chapters, you'll understand why certain investments might be better for your goals and risk tolerance. You'll see why it's usually wiser to own lots of different things rather than gambling on a few, why you should care about inflation's impact, and why having some investments easier to access matters even if you're playing the long game.

Most importantly, these ideas empower you to take control of your money. Instead of just hoping your investments grow, you'll use diversification to reduce risk, inflation awareness to aim for real gains, and liquidity planning to avoid surprise emergencies. That's the kind of confident, calm approach that builds lasting wealth. And starting now, when you're young, means you have the most significant advantage to turn these concepts into wealth that lasts a lifetime.

Fun Fact:
Most impulse buys happen when we're bored, not when we actually need something!

Tax-Advantaged Accounts Basics: Roth IRA & More in Teen Language

So you've got the basics of investing down, and you're ready to get serious about growing your money. One of the smartest moves you can make early on is to use what are called "tax-advantaged accounts." Yeah, the phrase sounds like something adults say to sound official, but really, these accounts are designed to help your money grow faster by saving you from paying extra taxes. Think of it like a secret boost that lets your investments keep more of their gains.

Roth IRA Simplified

The most popular one you might hear about is the Roth IRA. It sounds complicated, but the idea is pretty simple: It's a special kind of retirement savings account where the money you put in can grow completely tax-free. That means when you're older and ready to retire, you can take out your money without paying Uncle Sam a dime on the profits. Pretty sweet deal, right? But to play by the rules, you have to use money you've already paid income tax on, which means you're putting in earned money from jobs, gigs, or hustles, not from gifts or other sources.

Because Roth IRAs grow tax-free, all the gains you earn over the years stay yours without getting sliced away by taxes later. It's like setting your future self up with a big reward party and no tax hangover.

Limitations

Now, there are limits, of course. You can only put in a certain amount each year, and to open one, you generally need some earned income. That means if you're making money from a part-time job, a side hustle, or babysitting, you're good to go. Also, Roth IRAs aren't just for retirement savings. Sure, you're supposed to leave the money until you're older, but you can actually take out the contributions (the original money you put in) anytime without penalties. That's a useful flexibility if an emergency or big life event pops up.

Traditional IRAs and 401(k)s

Besides Roth IRAs, there are other special accounts like Traditional IRAs and 401(k)s. A Traditional IRA is like a Roth IRA, but flipped:

you don't pay taxes when you put money in, but you do pay taxes when you take it out. A 401(k) usually comes from a job, and sometimes your boss adds extra money—free money! Since most teens don't have jobs with 401(k)s, Roth IRAs are usually easier to use.

These accounts are special because the government doesn't take taxes from the money while it grows. In a regular account, the government takes some of your earnings each year. In a Roth IRA or similar account, your money can grow without losing money to taxes, so you end up with more in the long run.

🚀 Health Savings Accounts

There's also the option of Health Savings Accounts (HSAs), which are another type of tax-advantaged account, but they're usually available to people with specific health insurance plans. HSAs are great because they triple tax-advantage your savings: money you put in is tax-deductible, it grows tax-free, and if used for qualified medical expenses, distributions are tax-free too. This makes HSAs a powerful tool for adults, but most teens won't be dealing with these right away.

Custodial Roth IRA

Opening a Roth IRA as a teen usually means teaming up with a parent because you're a minor. That's called a custodial Roth IRA. Your parent or guardian sets up and manages the account until you turn 18 or 21 (depending on the state), and then it's officially yours. You'll also need to show proof of income, so if you haven't started working yet, now's a good time to start thinking about gigs or part-time jobs. Even something small helps you get on the path to building big wealth.

Understand What Can Be Invested

A Roth IRA is like a special money box where your money can grow without paying taxes. Inside it, you can pick different things to invest in, like stocks, bonds, or funds. You get to choose what fits you and how much risk you want.

A smart way to start is with something simple, like a fund that spreads your money across lots of companies. This helps your money grow steadily and lowers risk.

Also, watch out for fees. Some accounts charge money just for using them, which can make your money grow slower. Look for an account with low or no fees so most of your money stays in your investments and grows for you.

Another tip is to contribute regularly, even if it's just $25 or $50 a month. The power of consistency beats trying to time the market or putting in big sums all at once. When you contribute regularly, you're practicing what's called "dollar-cost averaging," which helps protect you against market ups and downs. Plus, building a habit now means you're less likely to stop investing later in life.

It's important to remember that tax-advantaged accounts aren't a magic wand. They don't guarantee your investments will go up in value, but they do give you a solid, legal edge to keep more of what you earn. Combine that edge with patience, discipline, and smart investing, and you're creating a financial combo move that can turn a small investment into a mountain of wealth over 40, 50, or more years.

📚 Stay Informed

And yes, the long game is key. If you start at 16 with a Roth IRA and use it consistently, the effects compound like crazy by the time you hit your 30s and beyond. In contrast, someone starting in their late 20s or 30s has to work much harder to catch up. This is why getting familiar with these accounts now, even if you can't max them out just yet, is a huge advantage.

Start looking into which brokerage firms let teens open custodial Roth IRAs. Some platforms are super friendly to new investors and offer tons of tutorials and tools to help you learn as you go. You don't need to figure it all out at once. Even contributing just $50 a month can be an incredible start—remember, the goal is steady growth and building a habit.

Getting friendly with tax-advantaged accounts like the Roth IRA gives you one of the biggest power-ups to your investing journey. It's not just about saving money today, but about giving yourself a massive head start to build real wealth, the kind that can support big dreams, independence, and financial freedom. This might sound like grown-up stuff, but starting now means by the time you're 30, you could be way ahead of most adults who didn't start early.

So, if you're ready to make your money work smarter (not just harder), learning about tax-advantaged accounts and opening your first Roth IRA could easily be your smartest move yet.

What a Stock Actually Represents: Owning Tiny Pieces of Companies

When you hear the word "stock," it might just sound like a line on a financial chart or a fancy term adults throw around. But at its core, a stock is simply a way to own a small part of a company. Imagine a giant pizza, cut into hundreds or thousands of slices. Each slice is a piece of that pizza. If you own a slice, you own a little bit of the whole pizza. That's exactly how stocks work, but instead of pizza, it's a company. When you buy a stock, you're buying a tiny ownership stake in that business.

👑 Voting Power

This ownership means you get certain rights. For example, owning stock typically gives you voting power, even though your single share might not carry much weight on its own. When big decisions come up, like choosing company leaders or approving major changes, stockholders get to vote. It's like having a say in how the company runs, proportional to how many shares you own. So, the more stock you own, the louder your voice becomes.

Dividends

Aside from voting, stock ownership also brings you potential financial benefits. Companies can distribute profits to stockholders through dividends. Dividends are cash payments made regularly or occasionally, based on how well the company is doing. Not all companies pay dividends; some choose to reinvest their profits back into growing the business, but when they do, it's a way for you to earn income just by holding onto your shares.

What's fascinating is that owning stock means you're not just holding a piece of paper or pixels on a screen. You literally have a claim on a part of that company's assets and earnings. If the company grows, becomes more valuable, or earns higher profits, the shares you own can increase in value. On the flip side, if the company struggles or loses value, your stock might lose worth too. This risk-and-reward dynamic is core to investing.

Now, it's tempting to think of stocks as owning "the company" outright, but that's not the case unless you manage to buy 100% of it, which is rare and expensive. Instead, think of stocks as shared ownership in giant teams made up of thousands or millions of investors. Your stake might feel small in the grand scheme, but collectively, these tiny pieces add up to the value of the entire company. And over time, as the company succeeds, your piece benefits too.

💥 Fuels the Business

One important thing to understand is that companies issue stocks to raise money. When a company decides it needs funds to kick-start a new project, expand, or improve operations, it might sell shares to public investors. In exchange, investors give them cash, which the company can use to grow. In this way, investing directly helps fuel business development. You're not just hoping to make money; you're contributing to real-world growth and innovation.

Think of it like this: if you invest in a tech startup's stock, you're betting that their new app will become popular and profitable. If it does, the company's success could mean higher stock prices and dividends for you. If it doesn't, your stock might lose value. This connection between your ownership and the business performance is why understanding what a stock truly represents is key to smart investing.

Stocks come in different types, but the most common you'll hear about are common stocks and preferred stocks. Common stockholders generally have voting rights and may receive dividends, but their claims to the company's assets come last if something really goes wrong, such as bankruptcy. Preferred stockholders usually don't have voting rights but have priority for dividends and assets over common stockholders. While this might sound complicated, knowing this helps explain why different stocks carry different levels of risk and reward.

Stocks Are Liquid

Another cool thing about stocks is liquidity, which means you can easily buy or sell them on stock exchanges, like the New York Stock Exchange or Nasdaq. Because these markets exist, investors have a clear place to trade ownership in companies without waiting for long periods. Unlike some investments that lock your money up for years, owning stocks lets you move in and out of positions relatively quickly when needed. That said, just because you can sell anytime doesn't always mean you should, especially if your goal is long-term growth.

Think Long-Term

It's also useful to remember that owning a stock is just one part of your overall wealth-building plan. While stocks can be a powerful tool because of their growth potential, they do come with ups and downs. Prices can jump or drop based on how well the company performs, how the economy is doing, or even what people think might happen in the future. That's why learning to think long-term and not panic over daily price changes will help prevent emotional decisions that can hurt your money over time.

Watching a company's stock price move gives you a guess at how well the market thinks it will do. If investors are confident a company will grow or do well, there's usually more demand for its stock, pushing the price up. If people worry about the company's future, they might sell their shares, which could drive the price down. But remember, the stock price is not the company's actual worth on a daily basis; it reflects what buyers and sellers agree it's worth at a given moment, influenced by lots of emotions and news.

This means owning stock doesn't just feel like it belongs to one company; it's a ticket into the grand game of business, growth, and value-building. Unlike owning a product or savings account, a stock represents a partnership between you and a company. The goal is for this partnership to, over time, earn more money, grow in size, innovate, and reward shareholders like you.

Investing Is Like Growing a Garden

Your money grows best when you water it with time, patience, and consistency.

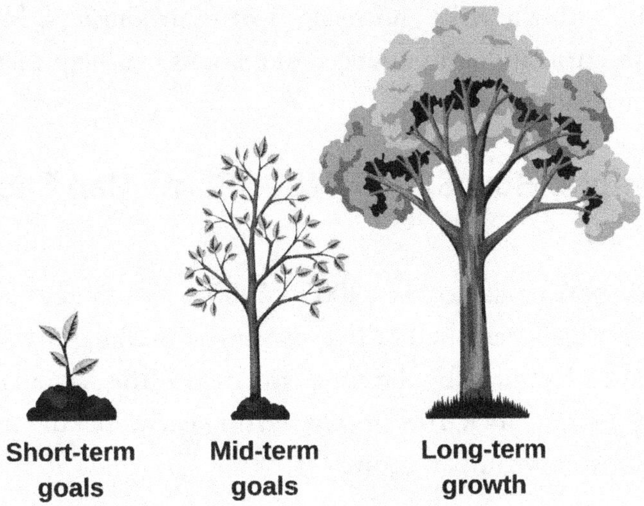

When you start investing young, buying stocks lets you become a part-owner of some of the biggest and most exciting companies in the world—the ones shaping tomorrow's technology, culture, and economy. Imagine owning a slice of a company that changes how we communicate, travel, or entertain ourselves. That's the power stocks bring. They open up more than just profit potential; they connect you to the exciting future that companies help build.

Ownership Comes with Responsibility

Lastly, it's good to recognize that stock ownership also comes with responsibility. Being a stockholder means keeping an eye on your investments, learning about the companies you support, and understanding how your money is working. Owning stock turns you into a mini-market participant, giving you opportunities to learn about economics, business, and money management firsthand. This knowledge will make you a smarter investor over time and help you build wealth more effectively.

In short, stocks are not some complicated Wall Street mystery. They're simple pieces of ownership in real companies that create products, hire employees, and try to make a profit. By owning these tiny pieces, you get to share in both the risks and rewards of their journeys. Hop into this world with curiosity and patience, and stocks can help turn your early savings into lasting wealth.

🤯 Example: How $200–$400/Month Can Become $1M by 30

If you start putting aside just $200 to $400 a month at 18 and invest it consistently, that steady habit can grow into something massive, possibly even around $1 million by the time you are 30. The secret is not luck or guessing the right stock. It is simply starting early, sticking to a plan, and giving your money time to grow.

Even $100 a month is better than waiting, and starting younger, like at 15, gives you an even bigger head start. What matters most is consistency. Investing a set amount every month is more powerful than throwing in random big chunks and then stopping.

You do not need to be perfect or rich. You just need to begin. Cutting a few small expenses here and there can free up the money to invest. Over time, those small choices can add up to life-changing wealth.

Beginner Portfolio Checklist

- ☐ **Start simple:** Don't try to buy a ton of random stocks. Begin with a few strong investments you can manage easily.
- ☐ **Build a solid foundation:** Think of stable stocks as the base of your portfolio. They give you a small piece of a good company.
- ☐ **Diversify wisely:** Spread your money across different industries and countries using broad-market index funds, instead of picking random stocks.
- ☐ **Avoid hype stocks:** Don't buy something just because it's trending on TikTok or YouTube. Focus on steady, long-term growth.
- ☐ **Start small and be consistent:** You don't need a lot of money to start. Even $50 or $100 each month works if you keep it up.
- ☐ **Include international exposure:** A mix of U.S. and international funds helps balance out ups and downs in the market.
- ☐ **Watch fees:** Low-cost funds are better because fees can eat into your money over time.
- ☐ **Learn before exploring individual stocks:** Focus on index funds first, then try individual stocks later when you're ready.
- ☐ **Be patient: Investing is a long-term game.** Let your money grow steadily over time without panicking at every market dip.
- ☐ **Avoid overcomplicating your portfolio:** Keep it simple, balanced, and easy to manage.

Final Thoughts

Summing it all up: You don't need 50 random stocks to start building real wealth. You need a simple starter portfolio made of broad, low-cost index funds that reflect the whole market. Keep the number of holdings small, pick quality funds, and stay consistent with your investments. This approach reduces risk, saves you time, and helps your money grow steadily across years and decades.

By focusing on this simple yet powerful foundation, you're setting yourself up for long-term success rather than chasing risky shortcuts. Remember, investing isn't about hitting a jackpot overnight. It's about creating steady, compounding growth that can lead to financial independence down the road.

So don't get overwhelmed by all the options or feel like you must jump in at full speed. Start small with a clear plan, choose simple funds, and stick with your strategy—even when the market is noisy. The habits you build now will pay off big time in the future.

Parents' Corner

Give your teen two jars. Label one Saving and the other Investing. Hand them any small items you have around the house, like coins, buttons, or candies.

Start by placing ten pieces in the Saving jar. Explain that this jar stays safe but grows very slowly. Then place ten pieces in the Investing jar and add two more pieces to show how investments can grow over time.

Every minute, add one more piece to the Investing jar and none to the Saving jar. Let your teen watch the difference build. After a few rounds, have them compare the jars and talk about why steady growth matters and why investing can be powerful over many years.

End by asking your teen to imagine what these jars would look like if they kept growing week after week. This simple visual exercise helps them grasp why starting early and staying consistent can lead to big results.

Key Takeaways

- **Investing Is for the Long Term:** It is about putting your money to work steadily over the years, not chasing quick wins or guessing which stock will explode.
- **Start Early and Be Consistent:** The earlier teens begin investing, the more time their money has to grow. Even small, regular contributions add up over time.
- **Investing Is Not Gambling:** Smart investing relies on research, strategy, and patience, not hype, luck, or short-term trends.
- **Understand Risk and Reward:** Investments can go up and down in value. Time and diversification help manage risk and reduce the impact of short-term losses.
- **Diversification Matters:** Spreading money across different stocks, funds, or assets reduces the risk of losing everything if one investment performs poorly.
- **Tax-Advantaged Accounts Give an Edge:** Accounts like Roth IRAs let teens grow money tax-free, making even small investments more powerful over the long term.

Dream Life Journal

Imagine you have $50 to start investing today. Write down how you would choose to invest it, what kind of account you would use, and how you think your money could grow over the next 10 years. Then reflect on what habits or choices you could start building now to make this growth even bigger.

🎓 Exercise: Your Investing Starter Sheet

Take a few minutes to reflect and make sure the big ideas actually stick.

1. What Does Investing Mean?

Explain investing like you're talking to a friend who thinks it's just "betting."

2. Time + Patience

If your $100 investment drops to $92 next week, how should you think about it if you're investing for years—not days?

3. Spread It Out

Give one example of a portfolio that is not diversified, and one that is. Which one feels safer, and why?

4. Prices Go Up

Pick something you love buying. How might its price change over time because of inflation?

5. Easy vs. Hard to Cash Out

Name one investment that's super easy to turn into cash and one that isn't. When might liquidity matter?

CHAPTER 6

Keeping It Stable: Balancing Risk with Strategy

"You must gain control over your money, or the lack of it will forever control you."

- Dave Ramsey

WHEN YOU START building your investment portfolio beyond stocks, bonds and REITs (real estate investment trusts) become valuable tools to add because they bring stability and diversity, two things every smart investor needs. Bonds are basically loans you give to companies or governments that pay you interest over time, offering a steadier, less risky return than stocks, which can fluctuate a lot. REITs let you invest in real estate without having to buy a house, meaning you can own pieces of apartments, malls, or offices while still keeping your money liquid and accessible.

Together, these assets help balance your risk, smoothing out the ups and downs of the market so your money grows more reliably over the years. Understanding these building blocks early on makes it easier to build a portfolio that aligns with your long-term goals and helps you stay calm even when markets get wild. This chapter helps in understanding these tools in detail.

Don't rely on one plant, grow a whole garden of income!

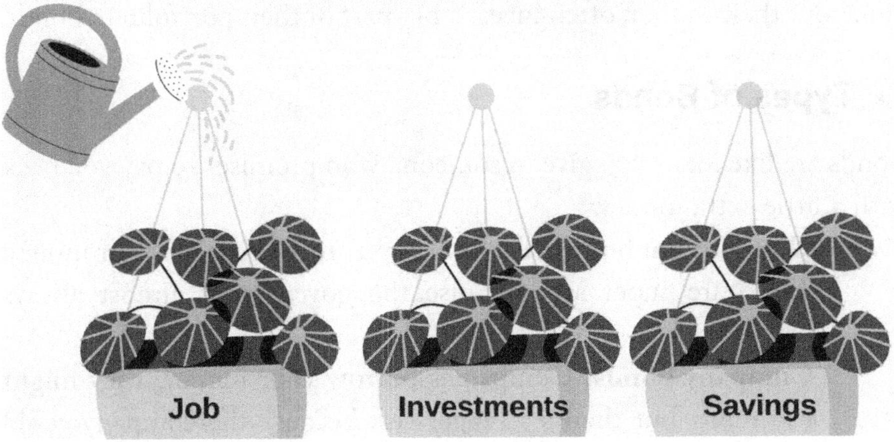

What Bonds Are and Why Grown-Ups Love Them

Bonds might sound boring compared to cool stocks or crypto, but they're really important for keeping your money safe while helping it grow. A bond is like a loan you give to a company, city, or the government. They promise to pay you back on a certain date (called the maturity date) and also give you extra money called interest along the way.

Bonds Are Considered Safe

Why do bonds get such a reputation as a "safe" investment? It's because bonds tend to deliver smaller, steadier returns than stocks, but they come with less risk. Stocks can jump up and down a lot—one day you're excited because your favorite company's stock price doubled, and the next day you might lose half of that. Bonds don't usually behave like that. Instead, they provide reliable interest payments that you can count on, so they're like the chill, dependable friend in your investment crew.

Think about it this way: if stocks are a roller coaster, bonds are the gentle train ride. You might not get the adrenaline rush of big gains, but you won't be thrown around as much by sudden drops. That's why grown-ups who are closer to retirement, or who just don't want to stress out about their money, often invest a big part of their portfolio in bonds.

👀 Types of Bonds

Bonds are like loans you give to someone who promises to pay you back with a little extra money.

- **Government bonds:** The U.S. government borrows your money. These are super safe because the government almost always pays it back.
- **Company bonds:** Companies borrow your money. They might pay more, but there's a bigger risk because the company could have problems or go out of business.
- **City or state bonds:** Cities or states borrow your money. Sometimes they give special tax perks, which can make them a good deal for some people.

> 💡 **Fun Fact**
>
> The bond market is valued at over $130 trillion, making it larger than the global stock market. While stocks often dominate financial news, bonds play a far more significant role in the global economy.

🗣 Understand Coupons

Now, let's talk about those interest payments, which are called "coupons" in bond-speak. When you buy a bond, the issuer agrees to pay you interest regularly, usually every six months. The rate they agree to pay is fixed upfront, so you know exactly how much to expect. This predictability is another big reason why bonds attract investors who want a more controlled income stream, whether that's for paying bills, saving for college, or just having peace of mind.

Because bonds usually pay interest twice a year, they can provide a steady flow of cash without you having to sell your investment. That's different from stocks, where you might get dividends but often only once a quarter or less. Bonds feel more like a paycheck from your money, which can be pretty comforting.

Less Volatile

Some people think bonds are boring, especially when they dream about getting rich fast with stocks or crypto. But bonds are like a safety net for your money. They make your investments less wobbly and protect your money when the stock market goes down.

Investing isn't just about making big money fast—it's about being smart and keeping your money safe. Bonds help with that. They might not make you rich overnight, but they keep your portfolio strong and steady so you don't lose a lot if the market crashes.

Fund Essential Projects

Another cool thing about bonds is that they're often used to fund essential projects. When the government issues bonds, that money can help build highways, schools, and hospitals. When companies issue bonds, they might use the funds to expand, hire workers, or develop new products. So, indirectly, your investment supports real-world progress.

For young investors like you, starting to understand bonds early is a smart move. Even though you'll probably focus more on stocks when you're first getting started because they offer bigger growth potential, knowing about bonds will help you make smarter decisions as you get older and start thinking about protecting your gains. Eventually, as you grow your portfolio, bonds will help you build a smoother, more balanced investment strategy.

Bonds Are Dynamic

Bond prices go up and down kind of like a seesaw. If new bonds pay more interest than your old bond, your old bond is worth less, so the price goes down. If new bonds pay less interest than your old bond, your old bond is worth more, so the price goes up.

But if you keep your bond until the end (the maturity date), you always get all the money you put in plus extra interest, no matter what happened to the price while you owned it.

To sum it up, bonds are an essential part of investing because they offer safety, steady income, and a way to balance out the risks from stocks. Grown-ups love bonds because they help protect wealth and provide peace of mind, especially when the market gets choppy. For young investors, knowing how bonds work means you're building a solid foundation for long-term financial success.

If you think about your investment portfolio as a team, stocks are like the fast players who score points quickly but sometimes mess up, while bonds are the steady defenders making sure the team doesn't lose ground. You need both to win the game of building wealth.

Bond Funds vs Individual Bonds: What Teens Need to Know

When you think about bonds, you might imagine lending money to a company or the government and getting regular interest back. That's called an individual bond. You know exactly who you're lending to and when you'll get your money back.

But there's another way to invest called bond funds. These are like a basket of many different bonds that lots of people put money into together. Bond funds make it easier for beginners, especially teens with smaller amounts of money, because you don't have to buy one big bond by yourself.

Individual bonds are simple to understand, but bond funds let you own lots of bonds at once, which can be safer and easier to manage.

Topic	Bond Funds	Individual Bonds
Diversification	Invest in many bonds at once, which spreads out risk across different companies, industries, and countries. A default in one bond has less impact.	All your money depends on one borrower. If that company or government struggles, your whole investment feels it.
Predictability	No fixed yield or timeline. The fund is always buying and selling bonds, so returns change day to day.	Has a clear maturity date. If you hold it to the end, you know when you get your principal back, assuming no default.
Control	Less control. The fund manager makes decisions, and the mix of bonds keeps shifting.	More control. You buy the bond, collect interest, and wait for maturity. Very "set it and forget it."
Minimum Investment	Usually much lower. Some funds let you start with around a hundred dollars or even less.	Often requires larger amounts. Many bonds are sold in thousand-dollar chunks.
Cost and Fees	Includes annual fees, called expense ratios. They're usually small but reduce returns over time.	May have higher upfront costs or trading fees, but no ongoing fund expenses.
Interest Rate Sensitivity	Prices adjust immediately when interest rates change, so the value can jump or drop any day.	Less sensitive if you plan to hold to maturity, since you'll still get your principal back unless the borrower defaults.
Liquidity	Easy to buy or sell on any trading day. Money is accessible fast.	Harder to sell early, especially with smaller issuers. You might need to accept a lower price to unload it.

Topic	Bond Funds	Individual Bonds
Taxes	Interest is usually taxed as ordinary income. Funds holding mixed bonds can get complicated. Good to hold in tax-advantaged accounts.	Similar tax rules. Some individual municipal bonds can be tax-free, but aren't always easy to buy when you're young.

So, what's the best choice for you as a teen just starting out? If you're looking for simplicity, easy access, and a way to diversify your fixed-income investments without requiring thousands of dollars, bond funds usually fit the bill. They allow you to own a slice of many bonds with a small investment, don't require you to pick individual bonds like a pro, and offer liquidity you'll appreciate if your financial situation or goals change.

On the other hand, if you understand the bond market well, can afford to invest larger amounts, and want predictable returns with a fixed maturity date, individual bonds might suit you better. They can be a solid way to build a safer part of your portfolio and reduce volatility. But as a teen, gaining enough knowledge and capital to make individual bonds work might be a longer-term goal rather than a first step.

Remember, the goal of adding bonds to your investing mix is to bring stability and balance. Stocks can be exciting, growing your money quickly, but they come with ups and downs. Bonds, whether individual or through funds, help smooth out those bumps because they usually pay steady interest and carry less risk. Choosing between bond funds and individual bonds comes down to your budget, how hands-on you want to be, your timeline, and your risk tolerance.

It's okay if you don't have all the answers right now. Starting with something manageable, like a low-cost bond fund inside a beginner investment account, means you're learning while growing your money. Over time, as your financial knowledge and resources grow, you can explore more bond strategies, including individual bonds if they fit your plan. The most important step is to add bonds to your portfolio thoughtfully, understanding their role in balancing risk and providing income.

Top 4 Common Investing Mistakes Teens Make

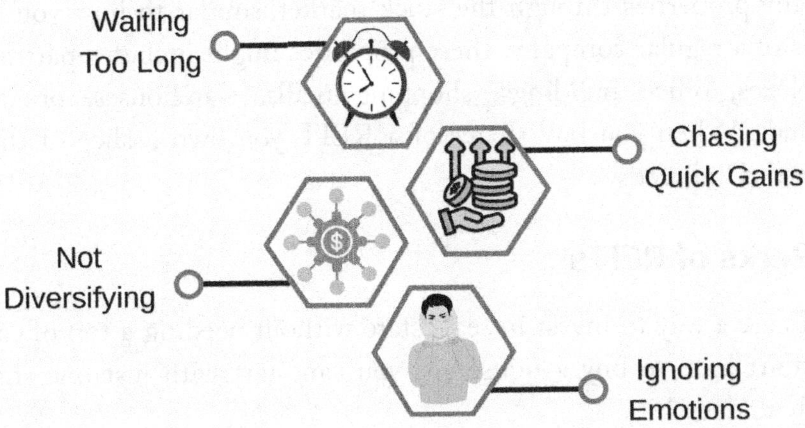

As you build your investing toolkit, keep asking questions about what you own, why you own it, and how it fits your goals. Bonds might not be as flashy as stocks or crypto, but they're a key part of the foundation that helps your portfolio weather storms and deliver steady progress. By knowing the pros and cons of bond funds versus individual bonds, you're setting yourself up to make smart choices now and smoother wealth building down the road.

🏠 REITs: Investing in Real Estate Without Owning a House

Real estate is often seen as a powerful way to build wealth. Buying a house or a rental property can generate income and an increase in value over time. But for most teens or young people just starting out, buying actual real estate isn't practical. Houses and commercial properties cost a lot of money, and managing them requires time, effort, and know-how. That's where REITs come in—Real Estate Investment Trusts let you invest in real estate without having to own or manage any physical property yourself.

A REIT is basically a company that owns, operates, or finances income-generating real estate. Think of it as a way to buy a small piece of many properties through the stock market, similar to how you buy shares of a regular company. These properties might include apartment complexes, office buildings, shopping malls, warehouses, or even hospitals. When you buy shares of a REIT, you own a slice of those properties indirectly.

🚀 Perks of REITs

REITs are a way to invest in real estate without needing a ton of cash. You don't have to buy a house . . . you can start with just one share, usually under $100.

They make money by collecting rent from tenants, and most of that money gets paid out to investors as dividends. You can spend this money or reinvest it to buy more shares.

The best part? REITs are easy to buy and sell on the stock market, unlike a house that can take months to sell and cost a bunch of fees.

REITs also help your money keep up with inflation. When prices go up, rents usually go up too, which can make the REIT earn more and pay bigger dividends over time.

Risks and Limitations

Of course, REITs aren't without risks. Like any stock, their value can fluctuate based on the stock market, overall economy, and the real estate market. If property values decline or vacancies rise, the income and share price might drop. Also, because REITs pay high dividends, they tend to retain less money to grow and reinvest, which can sometimes limit long-term stock price growth compared to other companies.

Easy to Manage

When compared to direct real estate ownership, REITs are far easier to manage. You don't have to worry about tenants, maintenance, repairs, or property taxes. Those responsibilities are handled by the company running the REIT. This hands-off approach is ideal for young investors who want exposure to real estate but don't have the time, expertise, or desire to be landlords.

Types of REITs

There are a few kinds of REITs:

- **Equity REITs** – They own buildings and make money from rent. These are the easiest to understand.
- **Mortgage REITs** – They lend money to people who own buildings and make money from interest.
- **Hybrid REITs** – They do a bit of both.

You can invest in REITs by buying one REIT stock or by using a REIT fund (like an ETF), which buys lots of different REITs for you. Funds are safer because if one building does badly, it won't ruin your money. For beginners, REIT funds are usually the easiest way to start.

🧐 Stay Informed about Tax Regulations

Since REIT dividends come with their own tax rules, it's good to learn how they affect your taxes. Unlike dividends from regular stocks, which are taxed at lower rates, most REIT dividends are taxed as ordinary income, which may mean paying more tax on them. This is important to keep in mind once you have your own income and file your taxes, especially if you're investing outside of tax-advantaged accounts like a Roth IRA.

So, why should you even consider adding REITs to your investment mix? The short answer: diversification. When you're young and just starting to invest, it's tempting to focus only on stocks because they're popular and easy to understand. But stocks and real estate often perform differently over time. Including REITs can balance out your portfolio, lowering overall risk and helping you ride out ups and downs in either market.

Because REITs provide income and potential growth, they're a great complement to stocks and bonds—the other main investment building blocks you'll encounter. Bonds tend to be safer but offer lower returns; stocks offer growth with higher risk; and REITs provide a mix of income and stability tied to real estate. This balance helps you build a portfolio that fits your risk tolerance and long-term goals.

Fun Fact:
Some Gen Z investors are using their stock profits to plant trees, turning "green" money into actual green

Invest Early

Remember, investing in REITs doesn't require perfect timing. Just like with stocks or bonds, the best approach is usually to start early and invest consistently, taking advantage of compound growth. Over years or decades, those dividends can add up, especially if you reinvest them. You'll start creating a flow of passive income that grows quietly in the background while you focus on school, work, or building other skills.

Finally, keep an eye on fees when selecting REITs or REIT funds. Some funds charge higher management fees than others, which can eat into your returns over time. Since fees compound just like earnings, finding low-cost options is smart, especially when your investment amounts are still small.

In summary, REITs offer a powerful way to invest in real estate without all the hassle of owning a property. They provide dividend income, portfolio diversification, and inflation protection, all accessible through the stock market with relatively low amounts of money. For teens and young people eager to build wealth early, REITs make real estate investing possible without the headaches and huge cost barriers. Add REITs to your toolkit alongside stocks and bonds, and you're building a smarter, more balanced portfolio for the long game.

Fun Fact:
Warren Buffett made 99% of his wealth after age 50, proof that patience really does pay off in investing!

Balancing is the Key

Wow... by now, you are practically an expert on investing. But let's get a gist of why we had this very important conversation on bonds and REITs in this chapter. This is because investing isn't just about chasing the hottest stock or crypto, but about finding the right mix. By spreading your money across different types of investments, you can grow your wealth while keeping things steady, avoiding big losses, and staying calm when the market gets bumpy. Bonds, REITs, and stocks all play different roles, and combining them wisely makes your portfolio stronger over time.

How Bonds, REITs, and Stocks Help

- *Diversification:* Mixing different types of investments reduces risk because they don't all move the same way.
- *Risk vs. Reward:* Higher risk can mean higher rewards, but balance with safer options like bonds and REITs keeps your money safer.
- *Timeline Matters:* When you're young, you can take more risk with stocks. As you get closer to goals (college, car, house), adding bonds and REITs protects your money.
- *Emotional Safety:* Bonds and REITs act like training wheels, helping you stay calm when the market swings.
- *Portfolio Construction:* Think of it like building a team: each type of investment has a different role, and together they work better than one alone.

📌 Final Thoughts

Balancing risk isn't about eliminating uncertainty; no investment can guarantee a win. Instead, it's about managing risk smartly and consistently, giving you the best shot at reaching your goals. Bonds and REITs add important layers to this strategy, serving as a safety net and income source without cramping your growth potential. Starting to understand and use these building blocks now sets you up not only for bigger gains but also for peace of mind as you build your financial future.

Parents' Corner

Sit with your teen and play a little "Build Your Own Portfolio" game using paper circles or coins. Label each one as stocks, bonds or REITs, then have your teen design three different portfolios: one focused on growth, one on safety and one balanced. Talk through how each mix would react if the stock market suddenly dropped or if interest rates rose. This turns what could feel abstract into a hands-on moment where both you and your teen explore how these building blocks shape a calmer and smarter investment journey.

Key Takeaways

- **Bonds Bring Stability:** They act like steady loans that pay interest and help keep your portfolio calm during market swings.
- **REITs Offer Real Estate Access:** They let you invest in property without buying or managing a building yourself.
- **Balance Reduces Stress:** Mixing stocks with bonds and REITs creates smoother long-term growth and helps manage emotional decisions.
- **Bond Funds Add Simplicity:** They give small investors instant diversification without needing thousands to buy individual bonds.
- **Interest and Dividends Matter:** Coupons from bonds and payouts from REITs create regular income you can reinvest.
- **Diversification Protects Goals:** These tools work together so you're not relying on a single type of investment to bear all the risk.

Dream Life Journal

Write about a time when something in your life felt unpredictable. If your emotions were a portfolio, which moments were "stocks," which were "bonds," and which were "REITs"? Explore how each played a part in keeping you steady or throwing you off balance.

🎓 Exercise: Build Your Mini Portfolio Map

Draw three circles on a blank page and label them Stocks, Bonds, and REITs. Inside each circle, write what you believe that investment is best at. Stocks might lean toward growth, bonds toward stability, and REITs toward income. After that, connect the circles with lines and explain how each one supports the others. This turns the chapter into a visual map you can understand at a glance and helps you see how these pieces work together to steady your financial future.

CHAPTER 7

Crypto & Digital Assets: Hype, Hope, and Hard Rules

> *"Financial freedom is freedom from fear."*
>
> **- Robert Kiyosaki**

CRYPTO AND DIGITAL assets have exploded in popularity, promising big gains and new ways to think about money, but they come with a mix of hype and harsh realities you need to understand before diving in. While the idea of owning digital coins or tokens sounds exciting, it's crucial to approach them like any investment, with caution and a clear plan. This means risking only a small percentage of your money, avoiding impulsive buys driven by hype or FOMO, and always asking tough questions about where the real value comes from.

The digital world is also full of scams, fake projects, and "get rich quick" schemes, so spotting red flags and doing your homework matters more than ever. Whether crypto lives up to its long-term potential or ends up just a passing fad, this chapter helps you protect your funds and adds a modern tool to your growing investment toolkit.

What Crypto Is in Plain English: Blockchains & Tokens

Crypto can feel like a whole new world, full of confusing words and flashy promises. But at its core, it's just a different way of storing and transferring value, like digital money that doesn't rely on banks or governments. To really get a grip on crypto, you need to understand two simple ideas: blockchains and tokens. These are the building blocks behind cryptocurrencies like Bitcoin, Ethereum, and many others you'll hear about.

📝 Blockchain

Think of a blockchain as a public digital ledger—imagine a notebook that everyone can see, but no one can erase or change what's already written down. Instead of one person holding the notebook, it's shared across thousands or even millions of computers worldwide. Every time someone sends crypto, buys a token, or performs any action on the system, a new entry is recorded in this notebook. Because the notebook is duplicated across many independent computers and constantly checked, it becomes almost impossible to cheat or commit fraud.

This is a pretty big deal. Normally, when you send money through a bank or apps like Venmo, those middlemen keep records and control your transaction. With blockchain, there's no middleman; the system itself is the record keeper. It's decentralized, meaning power and control aren't concentrated in one place. This transparency and security are why many people get excited about crypto, as it promises a way to transfer money and assets without relying on traditional institutions.

Tokens

Now, let's talk about tokens. These are the digital 'things' you can own or trade on various blockchains. The most famous token is Bitcoin, but there are thousands of others with different purposes. Some tokens represent digital money, others act as digital collectibles, and some even give you certain rights or access within an online platform. In simple terms, a token is just a piece of data on a blockchain that represents something valuable.

Token Type	Purpose	Examples/Use Cases
Cryptocurrencies	Designed primarily as money, it can be used to pay, save, or trade	Bitcoin, Litecoin
Utility Tokens	Provide access to a service or product within a crypto ecosystem	Accessing a decentralized app, voting on project decisions

One way to picture blockchain and tokens is to compare them to video games. Imagine your favorite game keeps track of every action you take, from leveling up to buying in-game items. Usually, all this data lives on the game developer's servers. If they shut down or change the rules, you could lose everything. But what if the game's data were stored on a blockchain instead? That way, every player could see all the game's data, and no single company could suddenly decide to wipe your progress or steal your items. In that light, crypto tokens are like unique game items or points that are yours no matter what.

⚖️ Consensus

Blockchains are like public, digital ledgers that everyone can see, but they need to make sure all the information is correct. That's where consensus comes in. Basically, all the computers running the blockchain have to agree on which transactions are real before adding them to the chain. To do this, blockchains use different systems:

⛏️ Proof of Work (like Bitcoin): Computers solve really hard puzzles to confirm transactions and earn rewards.

🏦 Proof of Stake: People with more coins get a bigger chance to check transactions.

These methods keep the blockchain secure and trustworthy.

Even though the mechanics can get technical, the takeaway is straightforward: blockchains create trust without trusted middlemen. This opens the door to all kinds of possibilities where trust used to be a major barrier. Sending money globally becomes faster and cheaper, smart contracts (which automatically execute agreements) become possible, and entirely new industries can be built without relying on traditional banks or centralized companies.

Tricky Aspects

Now, before you get caught up in the hype, it's important to know that crypto isn't magic money. Its value depends on how much people trust and use it, and the ecosystem is still pretty new and wild. Some tokens might be valuable for a long time, while others vanish quickly. Understanding what a token does and the problem it's trying to solve can help separate solid projects from hype-driven ones.

Another thing to remember is that blockchains come in different flavors. Bitcoin was the first and focuses mostly on being a digital currency. Ethereum, on the other hand, is more like a giant programmable computer that lets developers build decentralized apps and smart contracts on top of it. These apps can do anything from lending money without banks to creating digital art you can actually own (we call that NFTs). Knowing the basics of how different blockchains work will help you understand why some tokens might have extra features or risks.

The rise of tokens has led to new forms of ownership and investing as well. Instead of buying traditional stocks or bonds, you can trade or hold a variety of crypto assets. Some tokens represent ownership in a project, some provide income through rewards or dividends, and others might grant voting rights in the project's future. This makes crypto a totally new kind of investing playground, but also means you need to do your homework before jumping in.

👥 No Physical Existence

If you're thinking of starting with crypto, get comfortable with the idea of owning something digital that lives only on the internet. Unlike cash or stocks, there's no physical coin or paper certificate. Your tokens are stored in a digital wallet — an app where you control private keys, kind of like the password to your crypto. Losing access to your wallet is like losing your money, so security here is super important.

To wrap it up, both blockchains and tokens represent a fundamental shift in how value and trust work in the digital age. Instead of relying on big institutions, you can transact and own assets directly with people around the world, all of which are secured by the network itself. Understanding these basics gives you a solid foundation to learn more about specific cryptocurrencies, their risks, and the opportunities they offer for building wealth early.

So, when you hear about crypto tokens or blockchain technology next time, you'll know they aren't just buzzwords or fads. They're part of a rapidly evolving financial and tech landscape that might open up new ways for you to grow your money and participate in the future economy. Just remember: like any investment, it pays to learn the rules first before diving in.

> 💡 **Fun Fact**
>
> There are over 10,000 different cryptocurrencies. Bitcoin was the first cryptocurrency and remains the most well-known.

Safe Crypto Rules: Small Percentages, Long-Term, No FOMO

Jumping into crypto might seem thrilling at first; there are stories everywhere about young investors hitting it big overnight. But before you get caught up in the hype, it's important to approach cryptocurrency with a clear head and a smart strategy. Crypto markets are famous for their wild ups and downs, so if you treat it like a gamble instead of an investment, you're setting yourself up for stress, mistakes, or worse, losing more than you can afford. The best advice? Keep your crypto allocation small, think long-term, and ditch any fear of missing out.

🚧 Limit Your Investment

First, let's talk about percentages. You don't need to throw your entire savings into digital coins just because you heard of someone doubling their money in a few days. In fact, a safe and responsible rule is to limit your crypto investments to a small fraction of your overall portfolio, somewhere between 1% and 5%. Why so little? Because crypto, while exciting, is still highly unpredictable. Keeping your exposure low means that even if a coin crashes hard or disappears entirely, your overall financial life won't be devastated.

This small allocation isn't about being scared of crypto's potential; it's about managing risk intelligently. Imagine you have $1,000 to invest. Putting $10 or $50 of that into crypto can be a way to learn and participate without risking the safety net you've built in stocks, bonds, or savings. If crypto surges, that's a bonus. If it tanks, you won't feel the pain as deeply, and it won't derail your other financial goals.

Hold for Long-Term

Along with limiting what you put in, holding crypto for the long term is crucial. Many investors treat crypto like a lottery ticket, hoping for quick wins and selling the moment prices drop just a little. This kind of short-term thinking leads to emotional swings that kill returns. Instead, think of crypto as a small addition to your diversified portfolio that you should hold without fiddling every day. When you commit to this mindset, price swings become less scary, and you avoid the trap of panic-selling low or chasing hype high.

Long-term thinking also helps you avoid trading too often, which can incur fees or even tax consequences down the line. The reality is nobody knows how high or low a coin will go in the next week, month, or year. By focusing on the bigger picture and giving your investments time, you're more likely to ride out the volatility.

Steer Clear of FOMO

Now, let's address a big one: FOMO, or "fear of missing out." This feeling can push people into buying crypto just because "everyone else is doing it" or because of flashy headlines promising overnight riches. FOMO is a powerful emotion online, especially on social media, where people often flex their wins while hiding their losses. The truth is, you never have to jump into something just because it's trending.

Fun Fact:

Your brain reacts to money like it does to chocolate, both trigger the reward center!

Steering clear of FOMO means creating your own plan and sticking to it. Decide how much you're willing to risk with crypto before you start, and don't deviate based on hype. When a new coin pops up, or prices suddenly spike, pause and ask: "Does this fit into my strategy? Am I risking more than I'm comfortable with?" If the answer is no, don't buy. It's better to miss a short-term jump than to lose money chasing every trend.

Another side effect of FOMO is emotional investing, buying high because prices are rising and selling low when things dip. This reaction is a classic way people lose money in crypto. It's tough, but remember that staying calm and sticking to your plan are strengths, not weaknesses. Building wealth usually means making patient choices, even when it's tempting to act fast.

Let's be real: some crypto projects are bound to go nowhere or turn into scams. This is why it's critical to do your own research before investing in any coin or token. Avoid blindly following influencers or friends who hype up obscure projects without solid information. Investing, even in small amounts, should come with a basic understanding of what you're buying and why.

When you combine small percentages, a long-term mindset, and resistance to FOMO, you build a healthy approach to crypto that fits with your bigger financial picture. This isn't just advice for teens; it's a fundamental rule for anyone diving into digital assets. Crypto might be a new and exciting frontier, but the basics of smart investing don't change: don't risk what you can't afford to lose, and always think bigger than the headlines.

Finally, remember that crypto isn't a get-rich-quick scheme; it's a high-risk, sometimes volatile asset in a balanced portfolio. As you gain more experience and confidence in managing your money, you might learn to recognize quality projects and opportunities. Until then, treat crypto as a fun, speculative side bet within a broader plan focused on steady growth and long-term success.

By following these rules, you protect your future while still participating in the innovation that crypto promises. You'll learn lessons about markets, risk, and technology along the way, skills that will serve you well no matter how digital assets evolve. So keep your crypto small, your time horizon long, and your emotions steady. That's how smart money grows, today and tomorrow.

Spotting Red Flags: Scams, Rug Pulls, and "Too Good to Be True"

When you first step into the world of crypto and digital assets, it's easy to get swept up in the excitement of skyrocketing prices and jaw-dropping returns. But what you quickly learn is that the crypto space—while full of potential—also comes with a significant risk of scams and schemes designed to separate you from your money. The phrase "too good to be true" exists for a reason, especially here. If an investment promises crazy-high returns with little or no risk, it's a giant flashing warning sign that something's off.

That's why being able to spot red flags isn't just helpful; it's crucial. Unlike traditional investments like stocks or bonds, crypto operates in a largely unregulated environment. This often makes it easier for scammers to steal money and harder for victims to recover it. Recognizing these warning signs early can save you from losing your hard-earned cash and, more importantly, protect your confidence as you build money smarts that will last a lifetime.

Notable Red Flags

So, what kinds of red flags should you watch out for? One of the biggest giveaways is the promise of guaranteed returns. Every investment, whether it's crypto, stocks, or a business, carries risk. No one can guarantee you'll double your money overnight, or ever. If you see a project or an influencer claiming this, be extremely cautious. Scams often prey on emotions like fear of missing out (FOMO) and greed, making grand promises to lure people in.

Another common red flag is pressure tactics. You might come across messages urging you to "act now" or "invest before the opportunity closes." Scammers do this to rush you into making quick decisions without doing proper research. Remember, legit investments don't disappear suddenly, and real opportunities give you time to think, ask questions, and evaluate the risks. If someone is pressuring you to send money immediately, it's a major red flag.

Sometimes, scams come dressed in fancy packaging—professional websites, slick videos, and lots of celebrity endorsements. While a polished look can lend credibility, it doesn't mean the investment is safe. Always dig deeper than the surface. Check for real technology backing the project, transparent teams (not just anonymous social media profiles), and active communities that discuss both pros and cons honestly. If all you find are hype and vague promises, that's a recipe for trouble.

The infamous "rug pull" is a particular type of scam that's become common in decentralized finance (DeFi) and crypto projects. A rug pull happens when the people behind a project suddenly disappear with investors' money, leaving the asset worthless. This usually happens in coins or tokens created with no real product or value, relying solely on hype to attract buyers. Knowing how to spot early warning signs of rug pulls, like anonymous developers, lack of a clear roadmap, or suspiciously high liquidity lockup, is key to avoiding getting caught in one.

Social proof is another area to examine carefully. Many scams use fake testimonials or bots posing as satisfied investors. These can appear in comments on social media, WhatsApp groups, or even YouTube videos. If you notice repeated phrases or overly positive reviews that don't address any challenges or risks, treat that as a red flag. Authentic communities aren't afraid to discuss problems, so silence or too much perfection is suspicious.

Learning to research a project thoroughly helps you go beyond hype and flashy marketing. Check if independent sources or reputable crypto journalists are covering the project. Look up publicly available audits of the project's code to see whether security experts found vulnerabilities or dishonest practices. If these audits don't exist or are incomplete, stay cautious. Remember, even audits aren't foolproof, but they add a layer of credibility.

A less obvious but equally dangerous trap involves "pump and dump" schemes. Here, groups of people artificially inflate the price of a cryptocurrency by buying a lot at once and promoting it heavily, often in private chats or forums. When prices spike, insiders sell their coins quickly, causing the value to crash and leaving others with losses. Learning how these patterns work and where to find honest price data can keep you from riding the wave up only to crash hard on the way down.

Beware of complex language and vague explanations, too. Scammers often use confusing jargon or buzzwords to make their projects sound sophisticated and legit. If an explanation of how a crypto project works is hard to understand even after some research, that might be a red flag. True innovations in finance can be complex, sure, but they're also usually explained clearly by people passionate about helping others understand them—not to confuse you so you won't ask questions.

Another subtle but important warning sign comes from how a project handles communication and customer support. If you can't find reliable contact information, responses are slow or non-existent, or information changes frequently without explanation, think twice. Transparency and accountability are fundamental to trustworthy projects. If teams vanish when investors have questions, that's a serious problem.

Sometimes scams come disguised as "free" or super-low-cost opportunities. For example, a project might offer a "free" token airdrop or a tiny investment with the promise of massive future value. But these often come with hidden conditions, like needing to connect your wallet to suspicious apps or paying high fees before cashing out. Always research what you're agreeing to before clicking or signing anything in your digital wallet.

In this digital age, scams can also show up as impersonations. Fake social media accounts or email messages pretending to be official crypto platforms or influencers try to trick you into sharing private keys, passwords, or recovery phrases. Never share this information. No real company or legitimate project will ever ask for it directly. Becoming comfortable with what information is private and how to protect it is part of building your financial defense system.

Learn from Stories

One way to build confidence in spotting scams is by learning from stories of those who have been scammed. These tales often share common themes: promise of quick wealth, missing details about the product, pushy sales tactics, and lack of transparency. These stories might sound like something you'd never fall for—until you realize the scammers used psychological tricks you didn't recognize at the time.

💡 **Fun Fact**

Bitcoin has a maximum supply of 21 million coins. This capped supply creates scarcity, which can help support its value over time.

🧐 Healthy Skepticism

There's no magic bullet to avoid all scams, but the good news is you don't have to be an expert coder or financial guru to be cautious and smart. Developing a healthy skepticism, asking tough questions, and taking time to research before handing over any money are your best tools. Always keep in mind that if someone is trying to get your money fast, and their offer sounds unbelievable, the odds are it's a trap designed to fail you.

Remember also that making mistakes is part of learning. If you encounter suspicious projects or feel you've been close to being scammed, don't get discouraged. Use those experiences to build sharper instincts and smarter habits. Over time, you'll develop the confidence to navigate both the excitement and the dangers of the crypto world with a clear head.

Finally, it's worth mentioning that protecting yourself is about more than just spotting scams; it's also about managing your own emotions. FOMO, or the fear of missing out, often clouds judgment and prompts people to make risky decisions. When you see a coin exploding in price, take a deep breath before jumping in. Real wealth takes time and patience. The gains that feel "too good to be true" often disappear just as fast as they arrive, while steady, informed investing builds lasting wealth over the years.

📌 Final Thoughts

Stay vigilant, do your homework, and maintain a healthy dose of skepticism. By carefully researching opportunities and questioning anything that seems too good to be true, you position yourself to recognize deals that are genuinely valuable—and genuinely safe. At the same time, avoiding scams, frauds, and "rug pulls" protects your hard-earned money from unnecessary loss. This approach not only safeguards your financial future but also allows your investments to grow steadily and responsibly, keeping you on track toward your long-term goals.

Parents' Corner

Turn it into a quick hands-on game. Give your teen a tiny imaginary budget and let them play Crypto Detective. They explore real projects, tag any hype or guaranteed return claims as red flags, and decide how they'd protect a digital wallet. The goal is to spot scams, notice FOMO feelings, and practice slow thoughtful choices. It keeps the fun of crypto while training the instincts that matter when real money enters the picture.

Key Takeaways

- **Start with a Plan:** Approach crypto and digital assets with a clear strategy, knowing how much you're willing to risk and how it fits into your overall portfolio.
- **Limit Exposure:** Only invest a small percentage of your money in crypto to protect your savings from high volatility and potential losses.
- **Stay Calm and Patient:** Avoid panic selling or chasing trends; treat crypto as a long-term addition, not a quick-money scheme.
- **Spot Red Flags:** Be skeptical of guaranteed returns, pressure tactics, or projects with little transparency—they're often scams.
- **Protect Your Digital Wallets:** Use strong passwords, enable two-factor authentication, and never share private keys to secure your investments.

- **Do Your Homework:** Research every project thoroughly, understand its purpose, and evaluate whether it aligns with your goals before investing.

Dream Life Journal

Imagine you invested $50 in crypto a year ago. Write a letter to your past self explaining what worked, what mistakes you avoided, and the lessons you learned about patience, research, and protecting your money.

🎓 Exercise: Crypto Decision Maze

Practice spotting crypto red flags and making smart investment choices.

Instructions:

Below are four crypto opportunities. For each, decide **Yes (safe to invest) or No (too risky)** and explain why.

5. A coin promising 1000% returns overnight, promoted by anonymous influencers.
   - Decision: ________________
   - Reason: ____
6. A small, well-documented token with a clear roadmap and active developer team.
   - Decision: ________________
   - Reason: ____
7. An airdrop that requires sharing your wallet's private key to claim tokens.
   - Decision: ________________
   - Reason: ____
8. A project with vague promises, no audits, and a "buy now before it's gone" email.
   - Decision: ________________
   - Reason: ____

Reflection: Which opportunities were easy to spot as risky? How will you use these skills when you encounter crypto in real life?

____

____

____

____

CHAPTER 8

Protecting Your Future: Risk, Scams & Money Mistakes to Avoid

> ***"It's not the man who has too little, but the man who craves more, that is poor."***
>
> **– Seneca**

WHEN YOU'RE STARTING out with money and investing, the biggest threat isn't just losing cash; it's losing trust in yourself and the process because of avoidable mistakes or scams that seem too tempting to ignore. It's crucial to recognize that risk isn't about fear; it's about managing what you can control, such as using strong passwords, enabling two-factor authentication, and avoiding debt traps like buy-now-pay-later schemes or credit card overspending. Emotional reactions like FOMO or panic selling can wreck your progress faster than any market downturn, so building the habit of calm, informed decision-making is your best defense. The simplest way to protect your financial future is to stay educated, be skeptical of "get-rich-quick" promises, and be disciplined enough to say no to flashy impulse buys or risky shortcuts that promise instant results but rarely deliver. Remember, safeguarding your money isn't just about avoiding scams; it's about building habits that keep your goals on track and your wallet safe for the long haul.

This chapter will walk you through the most common money mistakes teens make—and more importantly, how to dodge them. From avoiding scams and debt traps to managing your emotions and staying secure online, every lesson here is about giving you the tools to take ownership of your finances. Mistakes will happen, but with knowledge, patience, and discipline, you'll be ready to handle them, keep growing your wealth, and build habits that last a lifetime.

Big Money Mistakes Teens Make and How to Dodge Them

Starting out with money as a teen is exciting, but it's also a minefield of common pitfalls that can derail your financial future if you're not careful. The truth is, mistakes happen, but learning what to avoid early on makes a huge difference. Some errors have bigger consequences than others, and by recognizing them now, you set yourself up to build wealth smarter and faster.

Jumping Headfirst into Trends

One of the biggest traps teens fall into is jumping headfirst into trends without understanding what they're getting into. Whether it's hype around a new cryptocurrency, a "can't miss" stock tip from a friend, or flashy get-rich-quick promises on social media, the excitement can cloud judgment. The key thing to remember is that no investment or money move is a guaranteed win, especially if you don't take the time to research and understand the risks involved. Acting on impulse rather than informed decisions can lead to losses that might take years to recover from.

Ignoring Budgeting and Falling into Debt Traps

Another surprisingly common mistake is failing to keep track of where the money actually goes. A teen might earn a paycheck or make some money from a side hustle but then blow it on instant gratification, whether that's clothes, gadgets, or nights out, without any thought toward saving or investing. Budgeting isn't the most thrilling topic, but ignoring it leaves you blindsided when bills come due or when you suddenly face opportunities to invest but don't have the funds ready. Creating a basic plan for needs, wants, and a future fund helps you avoid this mistake by making choices ahead of time.

Credit cards and debt are a huge stumbling block for many young people just starting out. It's easy to think, "I'll just pay it off later," or to be seduced by zero-interest offers and buy-now-pay-later schemes. The reality is that credit cards can quickly become debt traps. Teen credit card debt at high interest rates takes years to pay off, often costing more than the original purchases. Knowing when to say no and understanding how interest works saves you stress and protects your good credit score for the future. Keep in mind: building credit responsibly early is smart, but the moment you don't pay your balance in full, the financial damage begins.

The Spending Mindset Meter

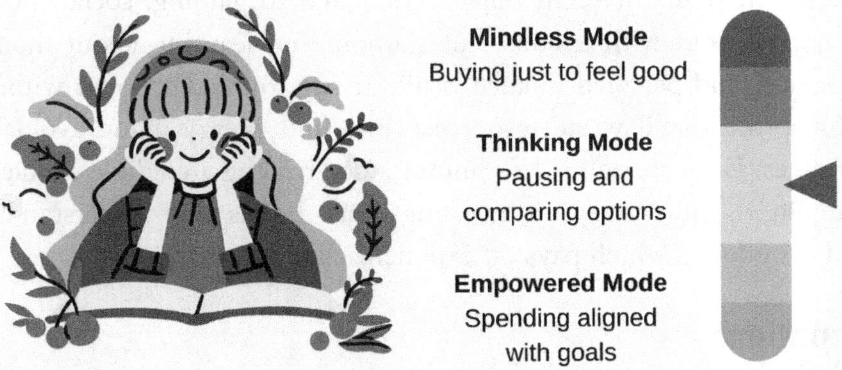

Having No Clear Plan

Investing without a clear plan or education is another big red flag. Many teens get overwhelmed by the thousands of stocks, cryptocurrencies, and other options out there. They might pick random stocks they overhear about or dump all their money into one "hot" investment, hoping for quick gains. This is gambling, not investing. Instead, starting with a simple, diversified portfolio and sticking to it prevents emotional decisions when markets swing. Keep it simple and consistent; this is where steady growth beats flashy wins every time.

One of the sneakiest mistakes is emotional investing. This means making money decisions based on fear, greed, or peer pressure. For example, FOMO (fear of missing out) might lead you to buy a crowded stock or crypto just because everyone else is. Or, in contrast, panic-selling when prices drop often locks in losses and misses out on rebounds. Avoiding emotional traps requires self-awareness and a solid strategy to rely on, not just trends or viral hype. This discipline takes practice, but it's essential for protecting your long-term progress.

Ignoring Financial Education

Another costly blunder worth mentioning is ignoring your financial education. It might seem boring compared to gaming, social media, or hanging out with friends, but skimping on learning about money, investing, and personal finance is like trying to build a house without a blueprint. You'll waste resources, time, and energy fixing avoidable mistakes. Even spending 15 minutes a day reading a credible article or watching a short video on investing basics builds your understanding and confidence, which pays off exponentially down the line.

Impatience

Most teens also underestimate the value of patience. Sometimes, impatience leads young investors to seek quick returns rather than focusing on consistent, long-term contributions to their accounts. Hitting it big overnight is rare and often comes with far greater risk. Embracing a mindset that prioritizes steady growth and trusts that time plays a major role helps avoid reckless bets and disappointment.

A related mistake is neglecting an emergency fund. When life throws curveballs, like unexpected expenses or income gaps, not having a financial cushion forces people to turn to high-interest debt or liquidate investments at bad times. Teens often overlook saving some cash for emergencies because it's less exciting than spending or investing. But an emergency fund protects your investments and keeps your path to wealth steady, so it's crucial to build even just a small one early on.

Constant Comparisons

Beware of "flexing" or trying to keep up appearances. Social media often showcases a highlight reel of others' lifestyles, and the pressure to match their spending or investments can be intense. Spending money to impress others, buying the latest gear, or jumping on every "cool" investment without your own due diligence is risky. Staying focused on your financial goals rather than comparisons helps you dodge this money mistake and keeps your financial house in order.

🌳 Developing a Cautious Mindset

Scams deserve a special call-out because they've become more sophisticated and aggressive, especially online, where teens spend a lot of time. From fake giveaways and impersonation scams to phishing attempts and bogus investment schemes, these traps can wipe out a young person's savings fast. Always question "too good to be true" offers, never share your personal or account info, and double-check any opportunity with a trusted adult or a credible source before jumping in. Developing a cautious mindset today pays off big in avoiding financial disaster.

4 Smart Ways to Protect Your Finances

One final, yet often overlooked mistake: neglecting to learn about fees and costs associated with investing. Many teens don't realize that brokerage platforms, mutual funds, and even some crypto wallets charge fees that chip away at returns. These small expenses add up to a massive total over the years. Understanding expense ratios, trading fees, and hidden charges helps you pick tools and investments that respect your hard-earned money rather than quietly eat it up. Low-cost options let your investments grow more efficiently, which is especially important when you're starting small.

In short, there's no magic bullet to instant wealth, not even the coolest app or trend. The biggest money mistakes come down to skipping education, rushing into hype, ignoring budgets, dabbling blindly, and falling prey to emotional and social pressures. But here's the good news: all of these mistakes are avoidable. By keeping a clear plan, staying patient, doing your homework, and focusing on consistency, you'll dodge these pitfalls and be well on your way to protecting and growing your financial future.

Fun Fact

Weak passwords remain a major security problem. Common choices like "123456" and "password" consistently rank among the most used and insecure passwords, leaving accounts vulnerable to hackers and putting both money and personal information at risk.

Take ownership early. Mistakes will happen, but the key is to learn fast, keep going, and never let a setback scare you out of building wealth. This way, when big decisions come your way, whether it's investing, managing debt, or spotting scams, you'll know what to do, so one misstep won't become a permanent setback.

Security Basics: Strong Passwords, 2FA, and Protecting Your Info

When you're just starting to build wealth and invest, protecting your financial information should be as important as learning how stocks or crypto work. You might feel invincible or think, "Why would anyone target me?" But the truth is, cybercrime and scams don't care whether you're a millionaire or just opening your first brokerage account. The earlier you lock down your online security, the safer your money and identity will be as you grow your investments.

Use Strong Passwords

It all begins with passwords. This might sound basic, but it's also where most people slip up. Using something easy, like "password123" or your pet's name combined with your birth year, is basically handing your accounts to hackers on a silver platter. A strong password is your first line of defense. What does that mean? Ideally, your password should be 12 characters or more and include a mix of uppercase and lowercase letters, numbers, and symbols. Think of it like creating a secret code that only you can remember, but that others can't guess.

One trick to creating strong passwords that you can actually remember is to use passphrases—combine random words or a line from a song with numbers or symbols. For example, "BlueStar$Moonlight82" is easier to recall than "j4f%9dl#q." Avoid cycling the same password across multiple accounts. That's like using one key for your house, your car, and your bank vault. If someone steals that key, they have access to everything. Password reuse is a top reason people get hacked.

Two-Factor Authentication

But even the strongest password isn't enough on its own. That's where two-factor authentication, or 2FA, comes in. You've probably seen apps or sites asking you for a code sent to your phone or generated by an authenticator app. That extra step might seem annoying, but it dramatically reduces the risk of a hacker gaining access to your accounts. Think of 2FA as your double lock; someone might find the key (your password), but they still need a second key, like a code from your phone, to get in.

There are different kinds of 2FA. The most common ones are SMS codes sent to your phone and authenticator apps like Google Authenticator or Authy. The app method is generally safer because text messages can be intercepted through certain hacks. Setting up 2FA usually takes just a few minutes for any account that deals with money—Brokerage apps, your bank, PayPal, and even your email. Remember, your email is the master key to resetting all your accounts, so protecting it with strong passwords and 2FA is essential.

Speaking of emails, phishing is one of the sneakiest and oldest tricks scammers use to steal your info. Phishing emails or texts pretend to be from real companies, asking you to "verify your account" or "confirm your password." They often include links that lead to fake websites designed to capture your login details. The best defense is never to click links from unfamiliar emails, especially if they create a sense of urgency like "Your account will be locked in 24 hours!" Instead, go directly to the app or website by typing the URL yourself, and check for suspicious activity through official channels.

Keep Your Devices Safe

Another important piece of the security puzzle is keeping your devices safe. Your phone and computer are gateways to your accounts, and if someone hacks these, they can bypass many of your defenses. Regularly update your software and apps because patches fix security flaws that hackers exploit. Avoid using public Wi-Fi for sensitive transactions without a VPN—a virtual private network encrypts your connection—otherwise, hackers on the same network can spy on what you're doing.

Many young people also use password managers to handle the chaos of dozens of complex passwords. These tools store, generate, and autofill strong passwords for you. They're a huge upgrade from sticky notes or browser-saved passwords, which are vulnerable to theft. By using a reputable password manager, you can have unique, random passwords for every site without needing to memorize them. Just make sure the master password for your manager is extremely strong and protected with 2FA.

Avoid Oversharing

It's also smart to think about what you share online. Oversharing your birthday, your pet's name, or even the street you live on can give hackers clues to guess your password or security questions. Social media is a great place to show off your skills and interests, but when it comes to personal info that could unlock your accounts, less is more. Scammers often comb through profiles to trick you or your friends into giving up sensitive info.

You'll hear plenty about how to make money, but protecting it is just as critical. Identity theft or stolen money can set back your financial goals by months or even years. If your accounts ever get compromised, act fast. Change your passwords, alert your bank or brokerage, and report fraud to the right authorities. Early action can save you from bigger headaches down the road.

Lastly, keep security top of mind as you add new investment tools or accounts. Whether it's a new crypto exchange, budgeting app, or digital wallet, take time to learn their security features and set them up properly before transferring any money. A moment spent setting up strong defenses now prevents regrets later.

Fun Fact

Encrypted connections using HTTPS offer a safer browsing experience by protecting your data from interception or manipulation. This ensures that sensitive information, like passwords or financial details, stays private and secure while online.

Having strong passwords, enabling 2FA, and guarding your personal info aren't just technical chores; they're fundamental habits that protect your future. Just as committing to investing regularly or budgeting your expenses is a small investment of time that pays massive dividends in peace of mind, so is security. Starting these habits early puts you a step ahead, ready to build wealth without unnecessary risks.

Saying No to Debt Traps: Credit Cards, BNPL, and Predatory Loans

Learning to say no to dangerous debt is possibly one of the smartest financial moves you'll make early on. As a young person eager to build wealth, avoiding debt traps isn't just about staying out of trouble today; it's about protecting your future freedom and keeping your money working for you, not for collectors or interest payments. Debt might seem like a shortcut to "get now, pay later," but it often turns into a slow, sneaky thief that steals your financial power.

Credit Card Traps

Credit cards can feel like a rite of passage, especially when friends start talking about their first card or those enticing "buy now, pay later" offers pop up online. It's easy to get pulled in by the idea of having access to cash that you don't technically have yet. But here's the catch: using credit cards or BNPL (Buy Now, Pay Later) options without discipline often leads to paying way more than what you originally spent. The interest rates on credit cards can be sky-high, sometimes 20% or more annually, which means a $100 purchase can easily balloon into $120 or more if you only make minimum payments.

Even worse, minimum payments can trick you into thinking you're handling your debt responsibly when, in reality, they mostly cover interest and barely shrink the balance. This extends the debt for months or even years. For a teen or young adult, that's wasted time—time you could've spent growing your money instead of shrinking your credit score. Let's be clear: credit cards themselves aren't inherently bad. They can help build a solid credit history if used wisely. The problem is, most young people get caught in the trap of spending money they don't have yet, thinking they'll "figure it out later."

The "figure it out later" approach rarely works as intended. Imagine owing money every month just to hold onto something that's already used up or outdated. And guess what? It's not just the credit cards; BNPL schemes are designed to hook you too. These payment plans break a big purchase into smaller, "manageable" payments you pay over weeks or months, without interest, until you miss a payment or can't afford the next installment. Suddenly, fees and penalties pile up, and what was supposed to be simple turns complicated and expensive.

Predatory Loans

Predatory loans take this concept one step further. You might have heard about payday loans or cash advances that promise quick cash when you're "in a pinch." These usually look innocent at first, but come with monstrous interest rates, sometimes over 400% APR. If someone recommends you take one because you need money fast, think twice. They're structured so you keep borrowing just to pay off past debt, trapping you in a cycle that's almost impossible to escape. Falling into one of these traps can torpedo your credit score, and worse, it drains your resources so fast that it crushes your chances to save or invest.

Debt grows when you keep feeding it with impulse spending.

Building Credit History

You may wonder, "If I avoid credit cards and loans altogether, how will I build a credit history? Don't I need credit to prove I'm trustworthy?" Great question. Building credit is important, but it's about how you use credit, not just having it. Instead of getting a credit card or loan impulsively, consider a secured credit card or a beginner card with a low limit and no annual fee. Make small purchases and pay them off in full every month. This way, you're showing lenders you're reliable without racking up debt. It's like training wheels; you don't have to speed, but you're learning balance.

On the flip side, banging the BNPL or credit card drums without a solid game plan is a recipe for disaster. Before you put anything on a card or sign up for installment payments, ask yourself: *Do I have the money saved or coming in soon to cover this easily? Is this purchase necessary right now, or can it wait?* Delaying gratification may sound boring, but it's a huge step toward controlling your money instead of letting it control you. This habit is the backbone of wealth creation.

Some people argue that credit cards and BNPL give them flexibility and rewards like cashback or points, and that's true if you're disciplined. But many teens and young adults haven't yet mastered the discipline. Just because you can buy something doesn't mean you should, especially if it puts your financial stability at risk. Rewards don't mean much if you're also paying hundreds of dollars in late fees and interest. Your goals of investing early and building wealth require you to view money as a tool, not an endless resource to swipe freely.

Fun Fact:

Paying off debt can actually boost your happiness levels, just like getting a raise!

Emotional Toll

Here's a reality check: The debt you don't take on today will be your investment capital tomorrow. The money you waste paying unnecessary interest hurts your ability to invest in stocks, bonds, or crypto assets that actually grow your net worth. And don't forget the emotional toll; dealing with debt stress can distract you from school, work, and building the skills needed to succeed financially. Managing mental energy is just as crucial as managing dollars.

So, how do you guard against these traps? First, stick to a budget. Allocate a specific amount for your discretionary spending and don't dip into your savings or investment cash for things that aren't urgent. This creates boundaries that keep impulse spending in check. Second, build an emergency fund—even a small one—so unexpected expenses don't force you to reach for credit. Third, stay skeptical of easy-credit offers online and in stores. If the deal feels too good or the payment terms aren't crystal clear, take a step back.

Educate Yourself

Another smart move is to educate yourself on how credit reports and scores work. When you understand what impacts your credit, like payment history, amounts owed, and length of credit history, you're better equipped to make informed choices. A good credit score doesn't come from how much you borrow; it comes from paying what you owe on time and keeping debt low relative to your credit limits.

Peer pressure can also lead you into debt. Watching friends buy the latest sneakers, gadgets, or clothes on credit might make you feel left out, but remember that appearances can be deceiving. Some might be sinking deeper into debt while keeping up a flashy image. Real financial independence comes from making choices that feel good for you in the long run, not from matching spending habits for social approval.

When shopping online or in stores, look for cash-back deals and discounts, or save patiently for high-ticket items instead of immediately opting for BNPL or credit cards. If you really want to build wealth early, practice delayed gratification daily, even on small things. It trains your brain, reinforces good habits, and reduces the risk of falling into debt traps.

Dealing with debt traps isn't just about avoiding financial meltdown; it's about building habits that make you a better money manager and investor. The sooner you learn to say no to these tempting but risky options, the quicker you'll grow your net worth. Remember, wealth isn't just about how much money you make; it's about how much you keep and grow.

📌 Final Thoughts

In conclusion, don't let credit cards, BNPL, or predatory loans lure you into spending money you don't have. Think of debt as a challenge, not a solution. Build a financial cushion, use credit cards only to build credit by paying them off in full, and keep your eyes open for sketchy loan offers. Your true power lies in controlling your money, not letting money control you. Risk, scams, and financial mistakes aren't just setbacks; they're detours from the path to your millionaire game plan. Saying no today means saying yes to a secure and wealthy future.

Parents' Corner

Encourage a conversation with your teen about common money mistakes by asking them to identify one financial decision they might face, such as choosing whether to buy something on a credit card, invest in a trending stock, or share personal information online.

Together, discuss the potential risks, emotional triggers like FOMO, and strategies to stay safe, such as budgeting, delaying purchases, and using strong passwords or two-factor authentication. This activity helps teens practice thinking through choices calmly and reinforces habits that protect their money and build long-term financial confidence.

🎯 Key Takeaways

- **Start with a Plan:** Always have a clear budget and investment strategy before spending or investing, so goals, not impulse, guide decisions.
- **Avoid Debt Traps:** Credit cards, BNPL schemes, and predatory loans can quickly erode your savings; only borrow when necessary and understand the terms.
- **Protect Your Accounts:** Use strong passwords and enable two-factor authentication to safeguard your money and personal information from cyber threats.

- **Stay Educated:** Continuously learn about money, investing, and financial tools to make informed choices and avoid common mistakes.
- **Manage Emotions:** Avoid letting FOMO, panic selling, or peer pressure drive financial decisions; take calm, deliberate actions to build long-term wealth.
- **Be Patient:** Focus on steady growth, maintain an emergency fund, and prioritize long-term goals over instant gratification for sustainable financial success.

Dream Life Journal

Imagine it's **10 years in the future** and you open your wallet (or check your bank account). Write a journal entry as your **future self** reflecting on the money choices you made as a teen.

Bonus twist: Give your future self a **fun nickname** like "Captain Savings" or "The Budget Ninja" and write as if you're narrating a story about your money journey.

🎓 Exercise: "Financial Obstacle Course"

Helps identify common money mistakes, practice smart choices, and navigate financial risks—all in a playful, hands-on way.

Time Needed: 15–25 minutes

Materials:

- Paper or index cards
- Pen/marker
- Optional: small coins or tokens to represent money

Step 1: Set Up the Course

1. On separate cards, write down **money challenges or "traps"** from the chapter. Examples:
   - ☐ "Click a link promising free money online."
   - ☐ "Impulse buy the latest gadget with a BNPL plan."
   - ☐ "Invest in a 'hot tip' without research."
   - ☐ "Use the same weak password for all accounts."
   - ☐ "Ignore your budget and spend all your allowance."
2. On another set of cards, write smart choices to dodge these traps:
   - ☐ "Do research before investing."
   - ☐ "Set up 2FA and strong passwords."
   - ☐ "Check your budget before spending."
   - ☐ "Wait 24 hours before a big purchase."
   - ☐ "Save for emergencies first."

Step 2: Navigate the Obstacle Course

- ☐ Shuffle the "trap" cards and place them face down.
- ☐ Shuffle the "smart choice" cards separately.

- ☐ The teen draws one trap card at a time and must **choose the correct smart choice** to dodge it.
- ☐ If they make the right smart choice, they earn a token (representing "safe money").
- ☐ If they pick incorrectly, discuss what could go wrong and how they could fix it.

Step 3: Reflection & Debrief

Ask questions like:

- Which trap felt most tempting or realistic for you?
- How did it feel to make the right choice and "protect your money"?
- What is one habit you want to start today to avoid traps in real life?

Outcome:

This exercise turns abstract lessons into a hands-on, memorable activity. Teens practice spotting risks, making calm, informed decisions, and reinforcing good habits—all in a playful "game" format.

CHAPTER 9

Your Millionaire-by-30 Game Plan

> ***"Too many people spend money they earned... to buy things they don't want... to impress people that they don't like."***
>
> **– Will Rogers**

GETTING TO A million dollars by age 30 isn't just a fantasy; it's a plan that you can map out and follow step by step, starting right now. The key is knowing exactly how much to invest each month based on when you begin, whether you're 13, 15, 18, or 21, and sticking with it through all the ups and downs life throws your way. This means setting clear targets, committing to regular investments, and reviewing your progress annually to tweak your strategy as needed.

Moreover, consistency beats timing every time, so focus on a routine that fits your life and keeps your money working hard for you, even through college, jobs, and income changes. Building wealth this way is less about luck and more about disciplined habits and smart decisions—and by following a solid game plan, the million-dollar milestone comes into sharp focus rather than a distant dream.

Therefore, this chapter focuses on helping you build that game plan. So, let's get started.

Action Plans by Starting Age: 13, 15, 18, 21

Starting early is the secret sauce of building serious wealth. The younger you begin, the more your money has time to grow, ride out market ups and downs, and multiply through time. But different ages come with different challenges and opportunities. Here's a tailored game plan for ages 13, 15, 18, and 21, to make sure you're setting yourself up right, no matter when you jump in. But remember, stay humble and smart, don't be the overconfident investor.

The following table shows how money skills grow from age thirteen to twenty-one, making it easier to understand what to focus on at each stage.

Age	What You Should Focus On	Income Ideas	Saving and Investing Steps	Key Skills to Build
13	Learning the basics of money. Understanding earning, saving, and spending.	Small jobs like babysitting, mowing lawns, or pet care.	Begin saving small amounts. Explore investing through books, videos, and simulation apps. Ask parents about a custodial account.	Curiosity about investing. Basic money habits. Understanding how effort connects to earning.
15	Growing independence with money. Increasing income streams.	Tutoring, graphic design, social media work, online selling, and local gigs.	Set automatic transfers to savings or investments. Build a small emergency fund. With parents, open a taxable brokerage account or start a Roth IRA if you have income.	Discipline with automatic saving. Understanding tax-free growth. Early portfolio awareness.
18	Making independent financial decisions. Building a real investment portfolio.	Internships, freelance work, part-time or full-time jobs.	Open your own investment accounts. Start simple portfolios with low-cost index funds. Apply for a credit card and use it responsibly. Avoid lifestyle inflation.	Credit building. Consistent investing. Understanding risk and asset mix.
21	Scaling financial habits and long-term planning.	Negotiating raises, job changes, side hustles, or small businesses.	Max out tax-advantaged accounts like IRAs or 401(k)s. Learn deeper concepts like asset allocation. Keep reinvesting and stay invested during market ups and downs.	Long-term discipline. Managing multiple income streams. Living below your means while growing investments.

Across all ages, the biggest common thread is consistency. It's not about how much you start with, but how often you show up with a clear plan and steady contributions. Your money needs time and fuel, regular investing and smart saving, to turn those early dollars into a million-dollar nest egg by 30.

Starting at 13 gives you the longest runway, but even starting at 21 can lead to big growth if you commit with focus and discipline. Each year you wait means more you have to save later to catch up, so getting started is non-negotiable if financial independence is your goal.

Equally important is the mindset at every age. Mistakes will happen, but the key is to learn from them quickly and adjust. Avoid flashy "get rich quick" schemes, understand risk, and keep your eye on real progress. Wealth isn't about luck; it's about smart decisions repeated over time.

One last thing: don't be afraid to ask for help. Talk to family members who know about money, seek out mentors, or join communities with the same goals. Being financially savvy early feels complicated, but with resources and support, it becomes much simpler and even fun.

Fun Fact:

If you save just $5 a day, you'll have over $1,800 in a year and even more if it earns interest!

💰 How Much to Aim to Invest Each Month for $1M by 30

Figuring out how much to invest each month to reach $1 million by age 30 might sound overwhelming, but it's simpler than it seems. The key is time and consistency. Starting earlier makes the monthly amount you need to save smaller, while waiting longer means you'll have to invest much more each month to reach the same goal.

For example, if you start at 18, you have 12 years to save. That could mean setting aside roughly $5,400 each month, which is clearly a big stretch for most young people. If you start earlier, like at 15, the monthly target drops to around $3,600. Start even younger, at 13, and you're looking at about $2,400 per month. Starting early gives you more room to build your savings steadily without stretching your budget too far.

If you wait until 21, your timeline shrinks to 9 years, meaning your monthly investment jumps to over $8,000. That's why beginning sooner is so important; it reduces stress and makes your goal feel more achievable.

The exact numbers don't have to be perfect. The real focus is on building the habit of consistent investing. Even if you can only put away $100 or $200 a month at first, it's more important to start than to wait for the "perfect" amount. As your income grows from jobs, side hustles, or raises, you can increase what you save each month.

Breaking your big goal into smaller, monthly targets makes planning easier. Ask yourself what changes you could make to hit that target: pick up extra work, spend less on non-essentials, or set aside a higher percentage of your income. The most important thing is consistency, saving regularly, even in small amounts, beats doing nothing while waiting for a windfall.

Fun Fact

The stock market crash of 1929 triggered the Great Depression, showing why financial regulations are so important.

The takeaway: start early, save consistently, and set a realistic monthly goal. Doing this helps you take control of your financial future, giving you freedom and options as you grow older.

Annual "Money Checkup": Reviewing, Rebalancing, and Adjusting

You've built a foundation by starting early and setting clear money goals, but your financial journey doesn't end once you open your first investment account. To truly grow your wealth and stay on track to hit that millionaire mark by 30, you need a yearly routine, a money checkup. Think of it like an annual health exam, but for your money. Skipping this checkup can lead to missed opportunities, overlooked risks, or worse, staying stuck in habits that no longer serve your goals.

Every year, your financial situation and the world around you will change, sometimes in small ways, sometimes in big ones. Maybe your income jumps thanks to a new job or side hustle, or maybe the stock market takes a hit and shakes up your portfolio. You might have new expenses like college or moving out, or you might discover a passion for a new investment type, like crypto. All of this means your plan can't stay static. It needs a refresh. That's where this annual review comes in.

A proper money checkup has three main parts: reviewing, rebalancing, and adjusting. Together, these steps keep you connected to your goals, make sure your investments stay aligned with your risk tolerance, and help you pivot when life throws curveballs. Without this process, it's easy to lose control over your finances, no matter how strong your initial plan was. Let's break down these parts so you can master this crucial yearly habit.

Reviewing: Taking Stock of Where You Stand

The first step is to look at the big picture simply. This means going through all your accounts—checking your savings, investments, cash flow, debts, and any other financial pieces you've got. Ask yourself: Am I saving and investing as much as I planned? How did my investments perform this past year? Did I hit any new financial milestones? What's coming up in the next 12 months?

Don't just look at numbers. Think about your mindset, too. Are you feeling more confident making money moves, or do some parts stress you out? What money habits have you built naturally, and where do you struggle? Recognizing these patterns helps you understand what's working and what needs tweaking. It's easy to ignore the less fun parts, like budgeting or debt, but getting honest about them is exactly how you avoid surprises later.

This step doesn't have to be overwhelming. Set aside a quiet afternoon, log in to your bank and investment apps, and write down key stats. How much have you earned? How much went into your investments? What's your portfolio value now? Did you stick to your budget? Track this over time, and this review becomes a snapshot of your financial health.

Rebalancing: Keeping Your Portfolio on Track

When you first started investing, you probably chose a mix of assets, stocks, bonds, maybe a little crypto, that fit your age and risk comfort. The idea behind rebalancing is to restore your portfolio to its original, balanced mix. Why? Because markets don't stay steady. Some investments will zoom up, others may drag or stay flat. Over time, this imbalance can increase your risk or shrink your growth potential.

Imagine your plan was 80% stocks and 20% bonds because you're young and want more growth. If stocks go on a big run, you might find that 90% of your money is now in stocks. That's riskier than your plan because you're more exposed to stock market drops. Rebalancing means selling some stocks and buying bonds to restore the 80/20 allocation. It's like steering your ship back on course when the wind pushes you off.

This doesn't mean you're timing the market or trying to guess what will happen next. It's about maintaining the risk level you're comfortable with. For teenagers and young adults, rebalancing usually means sticking to what you can emotionally handle and what aligns with your long-term growth goals, rather than chasing daily news or hype.

You can rebalance manually by selling and buying assets, or many online investment platforms have "auto-rebalancing" features to do this for you. Either way, making this a yearly habit keeps your investments working for you rather than against you.

Fun Fact:
Studies show that people who visualize abundance daily are 30% more likely to reach their financial goals!

Adjusting: Tweaking Your Strategy Based on Life Changes

Life moves fast in your teens and twenties. What felt perfect a year ago might not fit your new reality. Maybe you started a new job with a higher salary, so you can boost your monthly investment amount. Or school expenses popped up, so you need to pause or temporarily reduce contributions. Whatever the change, adjusting your plan means reflecting realistically on your current circumstances and future goals.

Adjusting also means updating your goals. Maybe you thought you wanted a million dollars by 30, but now you realize you want to retire early or travel the world. Your money moves should align with these evolving dreams, not rigidly stick to old plans just because you wrote them down. Flexibility lets your money serve your life—not the other way around.

Part of adjusting also means revisiting your emergency fund or debt situation each year. Your financial safety net should grow as your income or responsibilities increase. If you started an emergency fund three years ago, this annual review is a perfect time to boost it as rent, car insurance, and other costs increase.

> 💡 **Fun Fact**
>
> Warren Buffett, called the "Oracle of Omaha," is one of the most successful investors ever and is famous for promoting value investing.

Lastly, consider tax changes or new investment rules that might affect you. Every year, governments update tax laws that might open new savings options or close loopholes. Staying informed and adjusting your approach helps you keep more of your money working for you.

💰 How to Make Your Annual "Money Checkup" a Habit

Scheduling your money review at a consistent time every year is key. Many people pick their birthday or the start of the new year. Find a day when you can block off an hour or two without distraction. Prepare for your session by gathering passwords, account statements, and any financial notes you keep. This prep reduces stress and helps you focus.

In your review, keep a simple checklist: review goals, track progress, note wins and struggles, assess your investment mix, and make necessary adjustments. Write down your action steps and set reminders to follow through. It's this commitment to deliberate time with your finances that builds strong habits and keeps your wealth growing steadily.

Don't fall into the trap of "set it and forget it." Instead, treat your money like a living thing that needs care and attention. If you miss a year, don't beat yourself up; just get back on track as soon as possible. Over time, these yearly checkups become easier and faster because you learn what to look for and how to act.

Why This Matters More When You're Young

Starting these annual reviews early has a compound effect just like investing itself. By adjusting your plan yearly, you avoid losing time to bad habits, missed opportunities, or unexpected setbacks. Every correction you make, every extra dollar invested, and every safeguard you build adds up exponentially over the decades ahead.

The teenage and young adult years are also a perfect time to develop strong financial awareness and discipline. Learning to review your money regularly now prepares you to handle bigger challenges later, whether it's buying a house, starting a business, or simply protecting your financial independence.

Financial life isn't just about how much you make; it's about how well you manage what you have and wisely plan for what's ahead. The annual money checkup forces you to stay engaged with your money instead of drifting aimlessly or reacting emotionally to market noise.

In fact, mastering this habit signals a real shift, from being a passive spectator of your finances to becoming the confident pilot of your financial future. It's no longer about luck or guessing; it's about smart adjustments based on clear information and your personal goals.

Remember, building wealth is about consistency, patience, and smart choices over many years. This annual checkup is a simple, powerful tool that keeps your game plan sharp and your journey smooth, ensuring every step takes you closer to your millionaire dream by 30.

1. Set a specific date each year for your money checkup.
2. Gather your financial info: accounts, budgets, debts, and goals.
3. Review your progress honestly—celebrate wins and spot weak spots.
4. Check your investment allocation and rebalance as needed.
5. Adjust your goals and contributions based on life changes.
6. Update your emergency fund and plan for taxes or new financial rules.
7. Make notes and schedule follow-up actions.

Doing this won't just keep your money growing; it will build your confidence and financial skills. When you're 30, looking back at your steady years of checkups will show a picture of discipline and intentionality, key ingredients in turning your millionaire dream into reality.

Staying Consistent Through College, First Job, and Life Changes

Maintaining strong money habits over time is one of the biggest challenges for anyone aiming to build serious wealth, especially during the whirlwind years of college, landing your first real job, and the unpredictable changes that follow. These periods come packed with new responsibilities, fresh freedom, and sometimes financial chaos. What separates the people who make it to millionaire status by 30 from those who don't isn't just how much they earn or save but how consistently they stick to their plan when life gets complicated.

Stick to Your Financial Routine

When you're in college, your environment shifts drastically from the structured rhythm of high school. You have more autonomy but also more distractions. Friends, social life, moving to a new city, and sometimes part-time work all compete for your attention. It's tempting to sink into spending fast and saving slow, especially if you're around peers with different financial priorities. Sticking to your financial routine during this phase means treating your budget and investing as commitments, not options. Automate your contributions whenever possible; it helps you keep paying your future self first, no matter what else is going on.

At the same time, college is also a rare opportunity to build strong habits with less financial pressure. Your expenses might be predictable, and you likely have fewer bills than you will after graduation. Use this time to refine your system for tracking finances, reviewing goals, and understanding your investment risk tolerance. Think of it as setting up a financial operating system that's ready to run smoothly when you hit the workforce.

Prioritize Savings

But the real test of consistency comes once you land your first full-time job. Suddenly, you're earning a steady income, but for many, so are your expenses. Rent, utilities, student loans, transportation, maybe even supporting family members—these add layers of complexity to your finances. Also, the "first paycheck" excitement often tempts people to immediately inflate their lifestyle—new gadgets, dining out more, vacations. The trap here is thinking you deserve to spend big just because you earn more now.

Instead, prioritize locking in your savings and investing habits before boosting lifestyle expenses. This is your moment to solidify the foundation you've already built. Keep your automatic transfers going, ramp up your investments gradually, and treat extra income, like bonuses or tax refunds, as an opportunity to supercharge your goals, not an excuse to splurge. Staying consistent during this transition is less about depriving yourself and more about building the freedom to make choices without money stress down the road.

Stay Flexible

Life rarely follows a predictable path, though. Changes like moving to a new city, switching jobs, or unexpected emergencies test your financial discipline like nothing else. These situations can derail even the best plans if you aren't mentally and structurally prepared. The key here is flexibility without losing sight of consistency. Adjust your budget when necessary, scale back contributions temporarily if life throws a curveball, but never quit investing entirely. Remember, even small contributions during tough times keep the snowball rolling.

✅ Review Your Finances

Consistency also means regular check-ins with yourself and your plan. Make it a habit to review your finances at least once every few months. Are your investment allocations still aligned with your goals? Has your income or expense situation shifted? Are your financial goals still relevant, or do you need to tweak them? These money "checkups" keep you engaged and aware, helping prevent complacency and avoid unexpected slips over time.

One mistake to avoid is assuming your financial plan is set-it-and-forget-it just because you automated your savings and investments. Automation is powerful, but your life changes, and your financial strategy should too. For example, if you take a new job with a higher salary, it makes sense to increase your investment contributions. Conversely, if you're facing student debt or other obligations, dialing back temporarily while still staying consistent is better than stopping completely.

Developing the Right Mindset

Another important factor to keep in mind is the mindset during these phases of life. College and early career years often bring identity shifts and social pressure. You might find that your friends spend wildly on experiences or possessions that don't align with your goals. The temptation to conform can be strong, but financial consistency often requires swimming against the current, at least for a while. Focusing on your long-term vision can keep you grounded and motivated.

Remember that building wealth isn't about perfection; it's about persistence. Some months will be easier than others to stay on track.

You might miss a savings target or withdraw from your emergency fund. That's okay. What matters most is that you keep moving forward. Self-compassion and resilience are key qualities here. One slip-up isn't failure; it's part of the bigger journey.

📌 Final Thoughts

College, first jobs, and the surprises that come with those years are your training ground for long-term financial success. By building habits of saving, investing, and regularly checking your progress, you position yourself far ahead of those who never move beyond living paycheck to paycheck. Consistency in managing your money is your true advantage on the path to financial independence.

Remember, flexibility and consistency work together. Life will bring changes and unexpected challenges, but staying true to your financial habits allows you to adapt without losing sight of your goals. With this approach, you create a system that can not only withstand the ups and downs of early adulthood but thrive through them.

Parents' Corner

Encourage your teen to create a "Future Money Map" together. Start by picking a target age and financial goal, then map out steps from now until that age, including income ideas, saving habits, and potential investments. Make it fun by using colors, stickers, or drawings to mark milestones.

After finishing, discuss how each step connects to their future independence, and brainstorm ways the whole family can support consistent saving and smart money habits. This shared activity builds awareness, accountability, and excitement about long-term financial planning.

Key Takeaways

- **Start Early:** The sooner you begin saving and investing, the more manageable your financial goals become.
- **Consistency Matters:** Regular contributions, even small ones, are more effective than sporadic large amounts.
- **Set Clear Goals:** Knowing exactly what you're aiming for makes planning and tracking progress easier.
- **Review and Adjust:** Annual checkups help you stay on track, rebalance investments, and adapt to life changes.
- **Flexibility is Key:** Life will throw curveballs; adapt your plan without abandoning your financial habits.
- **Financial Knowledge Builds Confidence:** Learning about money, investing, and budgeting early sets you up for long-term success.

Dream Life Journal

If your money could talk, what would it say about how you treat it? Draw or write a conversation between your future millionaire self at 30 and your current self. What advice, warnings, or cheers does your future self give you about saving, investing, and staying consistent?

🎓 Exercise: My Million-Dollar Map

Instructions:

1. Choose your target age (e.g., 30) and your goal amount (e.g., $1 million).
2. Draw a timeline from your current age to your target age.
3. On the timeline, mark key milestones: when you'll start investing, when you expect income changes, and any savings goals.
4. Fill in your plan: include small income ideas, monthly savings, and investment steps for each milestone.

Age	Income Ideas	Monthly Savings Goal	Investment Steps	Notes / Adjustments

CHAPTER 10

Smart Money Moves During College and Early Adulthood

> *"The rich invest in time, the poor invest in money."*
>
> **– Warren Buffett**

COLLEGE AND EARLY adulthood bring a new level of financial freedom and responsibility that can feel overwhelming if you're not prepared, but smart money moves now set the stage for a lifetime of wealth-building. Managing money away from home means learning to budget for rent, groceries, and other essentials while handling irregular income from part-time jobs or internships without falling into debt traps.

Moreover, navigating student loans and scholarships requires careful planning to minimize borrowing and understand repayment options before interest piles up. Building credit responsibly by using credit cards or loans responsibly helps establish a strong financial foundation, giving you better terms on future loans and sending a positive signal to potential employers.

Ultimately, the key is to make thoughtful choices, automate where you can, and stay consistent, so your money works as hard as you do during these critical years. This chapter aims to enable you to make smart choices through strategic planning.

Managing Finances Away From Home

Leaving home, whether it's for college, a first job, or an internship, means stepping into a new world of financial responsibility. Suddenly, you're in charge of paying bills, buying groceries, managing rent, and handling your own money without the safety net of family support. This transition can feel overwhelming, but it's also a crucial step toward financial independence. Learning to manage your finances away from home creates habits that will stick with you well into adulthood and make the difference between living paycheck to paycheck and building lasting wealth.

💰 Understand Cost of Living

One of the first challenges is understanding your actual cost of living. When you're at home, many expenses are covered for you, such as meals, utilities, internet, and even laundry. Once you move out, these costs are charged directly to your bank account. Start by listing every monthly expense you'll face: rent, utilities, groceries, transportation, phone bills, subscriptions, and personal spending. This exercise isn't just about knowing numbers; it gives you a real sense of the money needed to sustain daily life. People often underestimate these costs or forget about smaller, recurring expenses, which can lead to money stress and overspending down the road.

Rent typically takes up the biggest chunk of your budget, so be realistic about what you can afford. The general rule of thumb is to keep housing expenses under 30% of your monthly income. If your rent would gobble up more than a third of what you earn, you might end up sacrificing other essentials—or worse, accumulating debt. When you're just starting out, consider shared housing options like roommates or university dorms. Splitting costs not only saves money but also makes it easier to build a social network in your new environment.

Beyond rent and utilities, groceries and other food costs can also spiral quickly. Cooking for yourself instead of eating out can save hundreds a month, but it requires some planning. Try writing a weekly meal plan with easy, affordable recipes. Bulk buying staples like rice, beans, and frozen vegetables reduces frequent trips to the store and curtails impulse purchases. The key here is balance. You don't have to become a gourmet chef overnight, but getting comfortable in the kitchen pays off in both health and savings.

Manage Cash Flow

Managing cash flow becomes trickier with irregular or infrequent income, which many students and young adults experience. You might get paid biweekly, monthly, or earn money sporadically through side gigs. Having a clear view of upcoming expenses and incoming cash helps prevent nasty surprises. Use a budgeting tool, spreadsheet, or even a simple notebook to track when money arrives and leaves your accounts. Identify fixed expenses—things you have to pay like rent and subscriptions—and variable expenses like clothing or entertainment, which can be adjusted in lean months.

Smart Ways to Outsmart Impulse Buying

Another part of managing finances away from home is understanding how to build and use an emergency fund in a new context. Your 'rainy day' savings become even more vital when you don't have parents footing unexpected bills. Whether it's a medical expense, last-minute travel, or replacing a broken laptop, emergencies happen frequently and unpredictably. Aim to build a cushion that covers three to six months of essential expenses. Start small if you must; it's more important to be consistent than to save a large sum all at once.

🏛 Understand Banking

Banking also looks different when you're on your own. Opening an account with low fees and easy access is a smart move early on. Many banks offer student accounts with perks like no minimum balance or free overdraft protection. Consider options that come with intuitive mobile apps and budgeting features; these make tracking spending simpler and less time-consuming. Automate bill payments or savings transfers whenever possible to avoid late fees and build good payment habits. Manual management might feel more hands-on, but automation prevents forgetfulness that leads to trouble.

Credit cards deserve special attention in this phase of your life. They're powerful tools when handled correctly; mismanaged, they can be the fastest way to sink into debt. Start by learning how credit works, but don't rush into applying for cards. If you do choose to get one, pick a card with no annual fee and a low interest rate. Use the card for small, regular purchases, like groceries or gas, and pay the balance in full monthly. This builds your credit history, which is crucial for future financial decisions, such as renting an apartment or buying a car. But remember, the line between using credit wisely and getting trapped by debt is thin.

Unexpected Personal Expenses

Living on your own also means handling unexpected personal expenses that rarely come up when you live with family. This could be replacing worn-out clothes, paying for new tech gadgets, or treating yourself to entertainment after a stressful week. Those “little” expenses add up fast if ignored. That’s why it's vital to allocate a portion of your budget to discretionary spending. This way, you avoid feeling guilty about enjoying life while staying on track financially. The balance between discipline and flexibility forms the foundation of long-term money management success.

👦🎓 Learn to Say No

Sometimes, managing money away from home also means learning to say 'no.' Peer pressure and social expectations might push you toward spending on things you don’t really need—going out every weekend, buying trendy clothes, or upgrading gadgets just because others do. This is where clear goals and a strong money mindset protect you. Keep your long-term financial visions front and center. Remind yourself that those small daily choices compound into massive differences over time. Saying no today might feel hard, but it's freeing when you realize freedom means having control over your money, not being controlled by it.

In addition to managing day-to-day expenses, early adulthood is the time to learn about taxes and financial paperwork. Filing taxes, understanding deductions, or even applying for financial aid or scholarships are tasks many young people overlook until it's urgent. Getting familiar with these processes minimizes stress and ensures you're not overpaying or missing out on money that's rightfully yours. Many colleges provide resources or workshops on these topics, so take advantage of them early.

Dealing with Student Loans

Another financial reality when away from home is dealing with student loans, scholarships, or work-study income, which you'll find addressed in detail later, but it's important to mention now that understanding your total financial picture is key. Don't let loans feel like a mysterious burden; educate yourself on repayment terms and how future payments fit into your budget. The earlier you get comfortable with these financial obligations, the better your odds of managing them without derailment. Remember, managing cash flow effectively today influences your creditworthiness tomorrow.

Making this transition successfully is all about building good habits that stick and staying curious about your finances. Every smart money decision you make while living independently, whether it's choosing a cheaper phone plan, cooking your own meals, or setting up a simple budget, helps build a foundation. This foundation supports bigger financial moves like investing, buying your first car, or saving for a down payment on a home later. Managing finances away from home isn't just about surviving; it's the start of thriving.

Here's a clear guide to help you navigate student loans, scholarships, and other financial aid while keeping your long-term money goals on track:

Topic	Key Points	Tips / Actions
Scholarships	Free money for academics, sports, community service, or talents; reduces future debt.	Research and apply regularly, including smaller or local scholarships; meet deadlines; write strong essays and gather recommendations.
Student Loans	Borrowed money that must be repaid; federal loans are usually better than private loans.	Borrow only what you need; understand interest rates and repayment terms; plan a repayment strategy.
Loan Management	Keep track of amounts owed, interest rates, and payment schedules.	Set reminders, create a repayment plan, and consider paying extra toward principal when possible.
Interest Awareness	Fixed vs. variable rates affect monthly payments and total cost.	Compare loan terms carefully before signing; avoid predatory lenders.
Additional Aid	Grants and work-study programs provide extra financial support.	Explore all options to reduce borrowing; track eligibility and application requirements.
Organization	Managing deadlines and documentation is crucial.	Use calendars, apps, or spreadsheets to track scholarships and loans; stay proactive and seek help when needed.

To wrap it up, the freedom that comes with living away from your family also means full responsibility for your money. That can feel heavy, but it is also empowering. Through understanding your expenses, creating a budget, building savings, managing credit, and preparing for taxes, you're sharpening the skills necessary to build wealth early. The lessons learned here lay the groundwork for every smart money move that follows. This phase might be tough, but with focus and consistency, your money will start working for you, not the other way around.

Budgeting with Irregular Income

Managing money gets trickier when your income isn't steady. Maybe you're hustling with side gigs, freelancing, or juggling work-study jobs in college. One week, you might bring home $200; the next, $800. That unpredictability can feel stressful, especially when bills and expenses don't wait. But here's the good news: having irregular income doesn't mean you're doomed to financial chaos. With the right approach, you can create a budget that flexes with your income swings while still keeping your long-term goals on track.

📝 Break Things Down into Essential Categories

The first step is to recognize that irregular income requires a different mindset. Unlike a regular paycheck that comes like clockwork, irregular cash hits your account sporadically. Treat each payday like a mini-budgeting cycle. Instead of planning expenses monthly based on a fixed number, break things down into essential categories—expenses that absolutely must get paid no matter what, and flexible or discretionary spending that can stretch or shrink depending on your current cash flow.

Start by figuring out your baseline monthly expenses. Think of essentials such as rent or dorm fees, groceries, phone bills, transportation, and minimum payments on any debts. These are non-negotiables; they keep your life running smoothly, and missing payments here can cause more trouble or extra fees that add up fast. Once you have a total baseline number, that's the minimum you need to cover every single month. Then divide that amount by four (for weeks) or roughly 30 (for days) to find your daily or weekly expense target. This small step breaks down big numbers into manageable chunks and helps you stay grounded when cash flow feels unreliable.

Buffer Fund

One trick to smooth over unpredictable income is to build what's sometimes called a 'buffer fund' or a 'running reserve.' If you get a good paycheck that's above your usual baseline, save the extra instead of spending it right away. This fund acts as a shock absorber during lean weeks or months when work slows (even putting away a little bit regularly can eventually create a cushion), reducing stress and preventing you from falling behind on bills. This habit is powerful because it builds stability out of unpredictability.

When you do get paid, treat your income like "paying yourself first," but adjust for irregularity. Instead of automatically saving a fixed dollar amount, focus on percentages. For example, you might save 20-30% of every paycheck you receive. That means on a $500 week, you save $100-$150, and on a $1,000 week, you save $200-$300. Over time, this proportional saving approach helps you build wealth steadily without feeling the pinch in weeks when you earn less.

Flexibility

Flexibility and prioritization go hand in hand with irregular income. One way to stay in control is to prioritize your spending using a tiered list. Essentials come first. Next, put some money toward paying yourself (savings and investment accounts), and finally, only after those, spend on wants or entertainment. This helps prevent a common money trap where fun or impulse purchases take priority over bills and savings, which can spiral into bigger problems over time.

It's also smart to get comfortable adjusting your spending habits week to week or month to month. If you know that one week you made less money than expected, consider cutting back on non-essentials—skip dining out, pause new clothes shopping, or limit streaming subscriptions for the time being. On the flip side, when income spikes, you could treat yourself a bit but still save a bulk of the extra funds. The mental shift here is to view your money as a flexible tool rather than something you need to lock into a rigid plan.

Record Keeping

Record keeping becomes crucial when your income fluctuates. Tracking every dollar helps you see patterns and understand your actual monthly needs. There are tons of budgeting apps designed for irregular income that let you mark income as it comes and track expenses in real time. With consistent tracking, you gain clarity about how much money you generally make and spend. This knowledge turns guesswork into data, which is vital for making informed spending and saving decisions.

Fun Fact

Keep all your receipts, invoices, and financial documents in one place. Using digital tools to scan and organize them can save time and prevent headaches when you need proof of payments, leases, or during tax season.

Avoid Overestimating

One pitfall to avoid is overestimating what you'll make in a given month. It's tempting to plan your budget around "best case" earnings, but this often leads to overspending and stress when reality falls short. Instead, use your lowest recent income month as a baseline. If you can cover your basics and save a little during the lean months, any additional money earned during better months feels like bonus fuel to accelerate your financial goals.

Another way to address irregular income is to prioritize "must-have" payments with fixed due dates before anything else. Some teens and young adults try to juggle everything at once, but focusing on rent, utilities, and minimum loan payments first reduces the chance of penalties or service interruptions. Once those essentials are accounted for, the variable part of your income can flow into savings, investments, or flexible spending categories.

📞 Communication is Key

Also, keep an open line of communication with anyone who's paying you irregularly, whether it's a boss, clients, or gig platforms. Clarify payment timelines to avoid surprises. When you know exactly when money's coming in, you can plan better and decrease anxiety. This simple habit can build professionalism and trust while sharpening your financial management.

Budgeting with irregular income is not just about keeping food on the table or paying bills; it's about creating a foundation that lets you invest and grow your wealth, even with unpredictable cash flow. That means once your baseline expenses and savings are secured, you can funnel "bonuses" or extra income into investing early. Starting young means your money has the maximum chance to compound and grow over time, even if you're earning sporadically.

Think of your budgeting process as a dynamic puzzle where pieces constantly shift. When you master adjusting your spending, saving, and investing based on cash on hand, you gain a massive advantage that many people with steady paychecks take for granted. Irregular income forces you to become more intentional, adaptive, and savvy about money. Those habits become lifelong skills that will pay off hugely long after school.

Finally, don't let irregular income discourage you from setting ambitious goals. Even if your income is all over the place now, the habits you build today—tracking meticulously, saving consistently by percentage, prioritizing essentials, and building a safety buffer—create a path forward. Over time, your money gets easier to manage, and you become more confident, all while staying focused on the bigger picture: investing early and building wealth that fuels your future freedom.

Fun Fact:
Warren Buffett made 99% of his wealth after age 50, proof that patience really does pay off in investing!

Building Credit Responsibly

Building credit might feel like one of those "adult things" you don't have to worry about just yet, but the truth is, starting early can make a huge difference down the road. When you handle credit responsibly during college and early adulthood, you're laying the groundwork for future goals, whether it's renting an apartment, financing a car, or eventually buying a house. Credit scores act like a financial report card that lenders, landlords, and even some employers check before saying yes to your requests. The better your score, the more likely you'll get better rates, approval, and opportunities. So, treating credit seriously now will save you money and stress later.

First, it's important to understand that credit isn't just about borrowing money; it's about proving you can borrow and pay back responsibly. This is often measured through your credit score, which considers your payment history, amounts owed, length of credit history, new credit inquiries, and the variety of credit types you have. Start simple by getting a credit card designed for beginners or students. Many banks offer cards with no annual fees and lower limits tailored for people with little or no credit history. Using this card smartly, like paying off your balance in full and on time every month, sends positive signals to the credit bureaus.

Pay Off Your Full Statement Balance

One common mistake is thinking you have to carry a balance to "build" credit. That's a myth. Carrying balances means you're paying interest and potentially digging yourself into debt. Instead, pay off your full statement balance every month. This keeps your credit utilization low (ideally under 30%), which helps boost your score. For example, if your credit limit is $500 and you charge $150, paying the full $150 before the due date is key. Consistency over time will grow your credit history and demonstrate reliability.

Start with One Card

It can be tempting to get multiple credit cards because "more cards = higher credit limit = better score," but that's a delicate balance. While having some credit diversity can help, opening lots of cards in a short period can backfire. Each time you apply for credit, a hard inquiry temporarily knocks off points from your score. Plus, if you're juggling more cards than you can manage, you risk missing payments or maxing out limits, both of which hurt your score. Start with one or two cards max, and keep the accounts open and in good standing for as long as possible.

👩‍💻 Authorized User

Besides credit cards, you can also build credit through other avenues, like becoming an authorized user on a parent's or trusted adult's credit card. This means their good payment history adds to your credit file, even though you're not the primary account holder. Just make sure the primary cardholder uses credit smartly, because if they miss payments or rack up debt, it reflects negatively on your credit, too. Another method is taking out a small credit-builder loan, where the lender holds the amount you borrow in a savings account while you make monthly payments. Once paid off, you get access to the funds, and your positive payment history gets reported, boosting your credit profile.

Avoid Debt Spirals

While it's crucial to build credit, it's even more vital to avoid the traps and debt spirals that can come with it. Credit cards can be powerful tools, but also dangerous if treated like free money. Overspending and then only paying the minimum due can lead to high-interest charges stacking up and your debt increasing faster than you expect. Always remember: the best credit strategy is one where you borrow only what you can afford to pay back in full and on time. If you use credit cards for routine expenses like gas or groceries, pay them off promptly and track your spending so habits don't get out of control.

Many young people also fall into the "buy now, pay later" (BNPL) trap, signing up for payment plans without fully understanding the consequences. While BNPL services can seem convenient, they can silently harm your credit if you miss payments, late fees pile up, or you take on more than you can handle financially. BNPL usually doesn't build your credit either, so it doesn't help your credit profile as a well-managed credit card does. Approach BNPL with caution, and always ask yourself if you can comfortably afford the payments before agreeing.

Another common question is: "If I don't have a job during college, how can I get approved for a credit card?" Some cards don't require proof of income but do require you to be able to repay debts. You might need a cosigner, typically a parent or guardian who agrees to pay back any debts if you don't, or you can start with a secured credit card. A secured card requires a cash deposit as collateral, which sets your credit limit and reduces the lender's risk. Using and paying off a secured card responsibly works exactly like a regular credit card and helps build a positive credit history.

📜 Check Reports Regularly

To maintain credit health, it's smart to check your credit reports regularly. You're entitled to a free credit report once a year from the three major credit bureaus: Equifax, Experian, and TransUnion. While checking your own report won't hurt your score, it helps you catch errors or signs of fraud quickly. Looking over where you might be over-utilizing credit or missing payments lets you course-correct before things spiral out of control. Some apps and websites even offer free credit monitoring tools, so you can stay updated without digging through reports manually.

Understanding how your credit score impacts your life is a key motivation to use credit wisely. A higher score can save you hundreds or even thousands of dollars over time in interest payments. Landlords often check your credit before renting to you, so a good score can mean better housing options. Employers in some industries also run credit checks, viewing financial responsibility as a sign of trustworthiness. Building credit responsibly isn't just about what you want now, but about opening doors for future opportunities that cost more than money.

> 💡 **Fun Fact**
>
> Credit Limit is the maximum amount you can borrow using your credit card. It varies based on your credit score and income.

It's also important to remember that credit building is a gradual process. You won't establish an excellent credit score overnight, so patience is necessary. Every on-time payment, every full balance paid, and every smart spending choice adds up. Avoid shortcuts like payday loans, which may charge sky-high interest and damage your credit if unpaid. Instead, focus on creating a simple system to track your bills, pay them on time, and keep your spending within your means.

Philanthropy and Giving Back

Listen now, this part is the most important. This is what makes everything worth it. Once you start building serious wealth, like passing that first million mark, it's natural to wonder what comes next. Beyond growing your investments and managing your finances, one powerful way to use your money is by giving back. Philanthropy isn't just for billionaires or celebrities; it's a mindset and a choice that anyone with resources can adopt. In fact, starting this habit early can shape your values and help you stay connected to what really matters as your wealth grows.

At its core, philanthropy means using your money, time, or influence to help others. It can be as simple as donating a small percentage of what you earn or volunteering your time for causes you care about. When you invest in other people or communities, you create ripple effects that go far beyond the dollar amount. Helping others can improve lives, support education, fight poverty, protect the environment, or fund medical research. But it also changes you; it builds empathy, gratitude, and a sense of purpose. When wealth is seen only as personal gain, it can feel empty. Adding generosity gives your financial journey deeper meaning.

📊 Set a Clear Budget

Giving back doesn't mean you have to be reckless with your money. It's smart to set clear boundaries and budgets for your philanthropy just like you do for personal expenses and investments. For example, you might decide to donate 5% or 10% of your income or returns. The exact number depends on your goals and situation, but the key is consistency. Making philanthropy a regular part of your financial routine can help turn giving into a lifelong habit. It's also motivating to track the impact you create; seeing the result of your contributions can feel more rewarding than just watching your balance grow.

Even Small Amount Counts

Sometimes young people hesitate to give when they're still building their own safety nets. That's understandable. But even small amounts can add up or help start projects. You don't need to wait until you're a millionaire to make a difference. For instance, micro-donations on social media or crowdfunding campaigns let you support causes with as little as a few dollars. Volunteering your time is another powerful way to contribute without spending money. Your skills, energy, and enthusiasm are valuable assets too.

Be Intentional

Another important side of philanthropy is being intentional about where and how you give. Not all charitable organizations or projects have the same impact. Some are highly efficient and transparent, using donations wisely. Others might spend less on their cause and more on marketing or overhead. Doing a bit of research, such as reading reviews, checking ratings, or asking questions, ensures your support actually goes where it's needed most. You can also explore "impact investing," in which your money is directed toward businesses or funds that generate social or environmental benefits alongside financial returns. This approach aligns your investments with your values, letting your wealth grow while pushing positive change.

Build a Legacy

Philanthropy also invites you to think long-term about legacy. When you envision building wealth beyond your first million, it's worth asking how you want to be remembered. Do you want your money to simply increase your lifestyle, or do you want it to improve the world in some way? Creating a legacy plan introduces the idea of stewardship—the responsibility to manage and distribute your assets wisely for future generations. This might mean setting up scholarships, funding community programs, or supporting causes that align with your passions. The earlier you start thinking about legacy, the more control you have over how your wealth shapes the future.

Giving back doesn't just flow in one direction, either. The act of helping others can bring unexpected benefits to you as well. Studies have shown that people who donate or volunteer tend to experience better mental and physical health, including lower stress and increased happiness. It can also expand your network in meaningful ways, connecting you with others who share your values and ambitions. These relationships can open opportunities you might not find through traditional investing or career paths. Philanthropy, in this sense, becomes an investment in your own personal growth and community.

Ways to Create a Legacy Beyond Money

Remember, philanthropy is not a competition or a status symbol. It's about genuinely caring and choosing to make a positive difference—big or small. Trying to outdo others or giving for the sake of appearances usually leads to frustration or burnout. Instead, focus on what feels authentic and manageable for you. Whether that means donating a few hours a month mentoring younger kids, creating content that raises awareness about a cause, or funding a local library, it all counts toward building a culture of generosity around your money.

Ultimately, building long-term wealth isn't just about how much you have, but what you do with it. Giving back is one of the smartest moves you can make, not only for others but also for your own growth and happiness. Embrace philanthropy as part of your financial journey, and you'll discover that true wealth is more than numbers – it's about impact.

Parents' Corner

Watching your teen manage money can be exciting and a little scary. Encourage open talks about budgeting, saving, and credit without taking over. Share your own money mistakes, cheer their wins, and let them solve their own problems. Celebrate each step toward independence, and remember: your role is guide, coach, and cheerleader, not personal ATM.

Final Thoughts

College and early adulthood are critical periods for taking charge of your finances. By learning to budget, manage irregular income, handle loans wisely, and build credit responsibly, you establish habits that set the stage for long-term financial stability and growth. The choices you make now, even small ones, compound over time, giving you control, freedom, and the foundation to build lasting wealth.

Key Takeaways

- **Budget Early:** Track all expenses, such as rent, groceries, and subscriptions, to understand your actual cost of living.
- **Handle Irregular Income Wisely:** Prioritize essentials, save a buffer, and adjust spending based on what you actually earn.
- **Build Credit Responsibly:** Start small, pay balances in full, and avoid debt traps like BNPL or payday loans.
- **Manage Student Loans and Aid:** Borrow only what you need, understand repayment terms, and take advantage of scholarships and grants.

- **Save for Emergencies:** Even a small fund provides security for unexpected expenses and reduces financial stress.
- **Make Intentional Choices:** Every financial decision—big or small—adds up over time, shaping long-term wealth and independence.

Dream Life Journal

If money grew on trees for one month, how would you spend it, and what would you save? Be creative, dream big, and then think about which choices would actually help you build real financial freedom in the future.

🎓 Exercise: Your First Personal Budget Challenge

1. List Your Expenses

Write down everything you spend money on in a typical month.

Expense Category	Item/Description	Amount ($)
Rent		
Groceries		
Transportation		
Subscriptions		
Entertainment		
Daily Purchases		
Other		
Total		

2. Track Your Income

Note all sources of money.

Income Source	Amount ($)
Job(s)	
Side Gig(s)	
Allowance/Scholarship	
Other	
Total	

3. Categorize & Prioritize

Category	Budgeted Amount ($)	Actual Spent ($)	Notes
Essentials			
Savings			
Flexible Spending			
Total			

4. Set Limits

Write your monthly limits for each category:

- Essentials: $_________
- Savings: $_________
- Flexible Spending: $_________

5. Reflect

At the end of the month, journal your observations:

CONCLUSION

Your Financial Journey Starts Now

> ***"It is a kind of spiritual snobbery that makes people think they can be happy without money."***
>
> **-Albert Camus**

SO HERE YOU are, at the starting line of what could be one of the most rewarding journeys of your life. Building wealth and mastering your money isn't just for adults who wander through complex financial jargon or for the lucky few born into money. It's something anyone can learn, especially if you start young, and the fact that you're reading this means you're already ahead of the game. What's exciting is that the tools, tips, and strategies you've picked up throughout this book are not just theories on paper but practical steps you can take right now. Your future self will thank you more than you can imagine.

It's easy to think that investing and managing money feels overwhelming, maybe even boring or confusing. But the truth is, breaking down these big concepts into small, manageable actions changes everything. Many teens never take the time to understand how money works, but you did. You've built the habits, mindset, and confidence that lead to real financial independence. Throughout this book, we've seen that wealth starts with how we think. A strong money mindset isn't about luck—it's about believing in opportunity, taking initiative, and choosing to build a better future for yourself one step at a time.

You've learned that financial literacy is one of the most powerful skills you can have. By understanding how to budget, save, invest, and avoid traps like high-interest debt, you take control of your financial life instead of leaving it to chance. These aren't just ideas—they're tools that help you make smart decisions, stay organized, and build long-term confidence.

We also explored the importance of starting early. Even small actions—saving a little each month, setting goals, or launching a side hustle—can grow into something much bigger over time. The sooner you begin, the more you benefit from compound interest and experience. You learned that investing isn't only for experts; it's simply owning a piece of something you believe in and letting your money grow while you focus on school, hobbies, and life.

At the same time, building wealth isn't just about earning—it's about protecting what you have. Knowing how to avoid scams, manage risk, and stay disciplined when things get tough gives you a major advantage. Smart habits like securing your accounts, paying yourself first, and planning for emergencies keep your finances strong and steady.

Most importantly, you discovered that money is a tool for freedom. When your financial choices line up with your goals—whether that's buying a car, paying for college, or starting a business—you create a life built on purpose. Wealth isn't measured just in dollars; it's measured in confidence, opportunities, and the ability to shape your own future.

As you move forward, keep these best practices in mind:

1. ***Pay yourself first.*** Save and invest before spending.
2. ***Set clear goals.*** Specific targets keep you focused and motivated.
3. ***Start early.*** Time is your greatest financial advantage.
4. ***Avoid bad debt.*** Don't borrow for things that lose value.
5. ***Keep learning.*** Financial knowledge grows just like money.
6. ***Protect what you earn.*** Use smart habits and security to stay safe.
7. ***Be resourceful.*** Earn creatively and turn your skills into opportunities.

Now it's your turn. You have everything you need to start building real wealth. Stay consistent, stay curious, and keep taking small steps every day. Every dollar saved, every smart choice made, every investment started moves you closer to financial freedom.

If this book helped you, share it with someone else who's ready to grow. Together, we can build a generation that's confident, empowered, and financially independent.

In the end, money isn't just about having more—it's about having choices. You have the power to create the future you want. Take that first step, stay committed, and watch your confidence and wealth grow. And now... there's a special surprise waiting for you on the next page. Go ahead—flip it!

Congratulations!
You've won a
BONUS BOOK

You did it!

YOU'VE REACHED THE END OF THE BOOK...

but the adventure doesn't have to stop here.

As a special thank-you for being such an awesome reader, you get exclusive access to a FREE bonus book... just for finishing this one.

Your Bonus Adventure is Waiting.

👉How to Get Your PDF:

1. Go to ***www.emmadavisbooks.com/freegift***
2. Sign in using your ***email address***.
3. Enter the ***unique code*** for your book.
4. Download your ***free PDF workbook*** instantly.

Use this code for your **free book**:

CJ7B93WJ

Please leave a

Review

Hi, can you help us out?
If you enjoyed this book, please take a moment to leave a review at:

emmadavisbooks.com
or
Amazon.com

Your review helps us reach more teens and the people who care about them—and keeps us inspired to create more books for you.
Thank you for your support!

Additional Resources

📚 Books to Inspire Growth and Financial Literacy

- **Mindset: The New Psychology of Success by Carol S. Dweck** This foundational book explains the idea of a growth mindset and highlights how believing in your ability to learn and improve can transform success.
- **The Total Money Makeover by Dave Ramsey** A practical guide to financial well-being that offers simple and direct advice on budgeting, saving, and paying off debt.

🌐 Online Courses and Guides

- **Growth Mindset for Parents** – Mindset Kit A free thirty-minute online course that helps parents understand growth mindset principles and how to use them to support their children's learning.
- **Growth Mindset for Parents –** Big Life Journal A short, easy to read guide with practical tips for building a growth mindset at home. It includes helpful examples such as effective praise and supportive language.
- **Fifteen Strategies for Cultivating a Growth Mindset for Teens** – Life Skills Advocate A detailed list of strategies that encourage teens to set achievable goals, face challenges with confidence, and view setbacks as learning opportunities.

Educational Tools and Kits

- **The Growth Mindset Workbook for Teens** – Social Workers Toolbox. A collection of forty activities designed to help teens identify strengths, set goals, and develop healthier relationships while strengthening a growth mindset.
- **TED Talk:** "The Power of Believing That You Can Improve" by Carol S. Dweck. A short talk in which Dweck explains how mindset shapes learning and achievement, and how believing in your ability to grow can open the door to success.

Activities and Worksheets

- **Twenty Growth Mindset Activities for Kids** – Mental Health Center Kids. A set of engaging activities, including "Negative to Positive" and the "Success Iceberg," that help children and teens practice growth-oriented thinking.
- **Growth Mindset Resources for Parents and Kids** – The Social Emotional Teacher. A variety of worksheets, activity ideas, and conversation prompts created to support families in building and strengthening a growth mindset.

ABOUT THE AUTHOR

Emma Davis is a woman who wears many hats. She is a clinical social worker, a therapist, and a financial advisor, as well as the author of Effective Anger Management for Teens.

Her books are aimed at teenagers, covering a diverse range of topics, including life and coping skills, DBT techniques, finances, puberty, developing a growth mindset, and career planning. She focuses on the unique challenges faced by adolescents in their emotional and physiological development, empowering readers with a strong foundation for understanding.

Emma draws on experience and knowledge from all her roles, as well as her experience as a mother, to guide young people through the difficult stage of adolescence. She runs a therapy practice and financial education agency tailored to teenagers, and has worked with a diverse range of young people facing different practical and emotional challenges. She also runs several online courses on cultivating interpersonal skills, gratitude, happiness, and joy, as well as 10 residential care facilities for adults with disabilities and mental health challenges, which also informs her work.

Emma is married with 9 children between the ages of 3 and 22. She enjoys spending time with her family, practicing jiu jitsu, and developing her skills in photography.

To learn more about helping
teens with finances,
anger management,
mental health,
and future life planning
please join my newsletter!
at www.emmadavisbooks.com

GLOSSARY OF KEY INVESTING TERMS

TO GET A solid start on your investing journey, here is a glossary of key terms you'll hear over and over. These words are the building blocks of smart money decisions. Understanding them early saves you from confusion and keeps you confident as you dive deeper.

- **Asset:** Anything valuable that you own, like stocks, bonds, cash, or even digital stuff like cryptocurrency. Assets can make you money over time.
- **Bonds:** Think of bonds like loans you give to companies or the government. They pay you interest, usually at regular intervals, and return your money after a certain period.
- **Compound Interest:** The magic of earning interest on top of interest. It's like a snowball effect that makes your money grow faster the longer you leave it alone.
- **Diversification:** Don't put all your eggs in one basket. Spreading your money across different assets helps reduce risk if one investment doesn't do well.
- **Dividend:** A payment some companies give shareholders from their profits. It's a way to earn money just for owning stock in those companies.
- **Inflation:** The rise in prices over time, meaning your money buys less than before. Investments need to grow faster than inflation to keep your buying power intact.
- **Liquidity:** How quickly and easily an asset can be turned into cash without losing value. Cash is super liquid, while things like real estate aren't.

- **Mutual Fund:** A fund that pools money from many investors to buy a mix of stocks, bonds, or other assets. It's an easy way to diversify, even with a small amount of money.
- **Portfolio:** Your collection of investments. It could include stocks, bonds, real estate, and maybe crypto, all working together toward your goals.
- **Risk:** The chance that your investment might lose value. Usually, higher risk means higher potential rewards, but also bigger chances of losing money.
- **Roth IRA:** A special retirement account where your money grows tax-free, and you can take it out without penalties in retirement. It's a powerful tool for long-term growth.
- **Shares (or Stock):** Owning a share means owning a piece of a company. If the company does well, the value of your shares usually goes up, and you might get dividends.
- **Stock Market:** A platform where people buy and sell shares of companies. Prices change based on demand, company performance, and the overall economy.
- **Volatility:** How much and how quickly an investment's price goes up and down. Higher volatility means the price swings a lot, which can be stressful but also offers big gains.
- **Yield:** The income return on an investment, often expressed as a percentage. For example, if a stock pays dividends, the dividend yield shows how much you earn compared to the stock price.
- **Crypto (Cryptocurrency):** Digital money secured by special technology called blockchain. Popular examples include Bitcoin and Ethereum. Crypto can be exciting, but it comes with a higher risk.
- **Emergency Fund:** Cash saved for unexpected expenses. It's stuff like an investment safety net, but in cash form, so you don't have to sell your investments in a pinch.

- **Index Fund:** A type of mutual fund or ETF that tries to match the performance of a whole market or sector, like all the companies in the S&P 500. It's a simple way to invest broadly.
- **Return:** The profit or loss you make on an investment. It includes both the money you earn and any change in the value of what you own.
- **Tax-Advantaged Account:** A savings or investment account with special tax rules that help your money grow faster, such as Roth IRAs or 401(k)s.

Diving into these terms now won't just prepare you for future chapters—it'll give your confidence a power-up. When you understand the language of investing, you control your money, not the other way around.

BIBLIOGRAPHY

Bach, D. (2016). *The Automatic Millionaire: Expanded and Updated – A Powerful One-Step Plan to Live and Finish Rich*. Crown Business.

Better Money Habits. (2019). *Personal Financial Education*. https://bettermoneyhabits.bankofamerica.com/en

For Investors. (n.d.). *FINRA*. Retrieved April 16, 2024, from http://www.finra.org/investors

Home. (n.d.). *Clark Howard*. https://clark.com

Investopedia. (2019). *Investopedia*. http://www.investopedia.com

Kiyosaki, R. T. (2017). *Rich Dad Poor Dad*. Plata Publishing.

LearnVest. (n.d.). LearnVest. Retrieved April 16, 2024, from https://www.learnvest.com

Mint. (n.d.). *Budget Tracker and Planner | Free Online Money Management | Mint*. https://mint.intuit.com

Money Crashers. (2018). *Money Crashers: Personal Finance Blog and Guide to Financial Fitness*. https://www.moneycrashers.com

MyMoney.gov. (n.d.). *MyMoney.gov*. https://www.mymoney.gov

NerdWallet. (n.d.). *NerdWallet: Make All the Right Money Moves*. http://nerdwallet.com

Orman, S. (2005). *The Money Book for the Young, Fabulous and Broke*. Riverhead Books.

Personal Finance | Life Skills. (n.d.). *Khan Academy*. https://www.khanacademy.org/college-careers-more/personal-finance

Ramsey, D. (2010). *The Total Money Makeover*. Nelson Current.

Ramsey, D., & Cruze, R. (2014). *Smart Money Smart Kids: Raising the Next Generation to Win with Money*. Lampo Press.

Sethi, R. (2020). *I Will Teach You to Be Rich: No Guilt, No Excuses, Just a Six-Week Program That Works*. Yellow Kite.

Siegel, F., & Crandall, R. (2004). *The Richest Man in Babylon for Today: New Secrets for Building Wealth in the 21st Century*. Grammaton Press.

Stanley, T. J. (1996). *The Millionaire Next Door*. Pocket Books.

The Balance. (n.d.). The Balance. https://www.thebalancemoney.com

The Motley Fool. (2020). The Motley Fool. https://www.fool.com

Wise Bread. (n.d.). *Wise Bread: Personal Finance and Frugal Living*. https://www.wisebread.com

Made in United States
North Haven, CT
04 November 2026

21760280R00124